Elvis

The Illustrated Biography

M·G·M

Elvis

The Illustrated Biography

MARIE CLAYTON

This is a Transatlantic Press book
First published in 2008

Transatlantic Press
38 Copthorne Road
Croxley Green, Hertfordshire
WD3 4AQ, UK

A catalogue record for this book is available from the British Library.
ISBN 978–0–9557949–1–9

Printed in China

Contents

Introduction

Elvis Presley was born in 1935, in very humble circumstances. He grew up in Memphis surrounded by black R&B as well as country and gospel music, all of which shaped his musical development. He burst onto the American music scene in 1956 with a sound unlike any other well-known singer of the time, and a sensual performing style that brought him many female fans—but also led to considerable criticism in the press. In person he was quiet and charming, but out on stage he moved in a way that drove women wild; he could belt out rock 'n' roll numbers, but sang gospel with real sincerity; he was polite and loved his mother, but his music appeared to encourage teenagers to rebel. Record sales rocketed on the back of all the publicity—and soon Elvis was one of the most popular singers in the world, earning millions but unable to step outside without causing a riot. The boy from nothing had grown up to become a living legend.

In 1958 Elvis was drafted, but he did his service in the US army without complaint or special treatment. The press quickly revised its opinion of him, and on his return home his new, more mature singing style brought him an even wider audience. However, rather than returning to the concert stage, for the next decade he concentrated on his acting career; all of Elvis's movies made money at the box office and he became the highest-paid actor of the time in Hollywood. He married Priscilla, a young girl he had met while in the army, and soon celebrated the birth of their daughter, Lisa Marie.

Elvis returned to performing live in concert in the 1970s, and his Las Vegas shows of this period were legendary. Unfortunately, his addiction to prescription drugs had started to affect his health, while his fondness for junk food had resulted in weight problems. Despite this, he kept up a punishing touring schedule, appearing live across America. Elvis died suddenly of heart failure on August 16, 1977, at home in his beloved Graceland, and thousands of fans gathered at his funeral. Today his musical legacy continues to captivate people—the annual Elvis tribute week in Memphis always draws crowds from around the globe. The King may be dead, but he lives on forever in the hearts of his many fans.

Chapter One

The Early Years

1935: A king is born

Opposite: Elvis Aaron Presley at around two years old, with his parents Gladys and Vernon. He was born on January 8, 1935. Gladys was very protective of her only son, particularly because Elvis's twin brother was stillborn. Elvis and his mother were unusually close—especially after Vernon was imprisoned for eight months for forging a check, leaving Gladys and three-year-old Elvis to fend for themselves.

Above: The two-room house in Tupelo, where Elvis was born, which was built by his father, Vernon. In following years the Presleys moved to various places around Mississippi, with both Vernon and Gladys working to support the family. Despite their problems, Gladys insisted that her son learn good manners, lessons that Elvis never forgot, even at the height of his fame. Gladys was closely involved with the Pentacostal church so Elvis grew up listening to live gospel music, as well as country and western on the radio.

A sense of rhythm and style

Left: Elvis remained close to his family throughout his life, sharing his success and acknowledging his debt to his parents. In one interview he said, "I never felt poor. There was always shoes to wear and food to eat—yet I knew there were things my parents did without just to make sure I was clothed and fed." Gladys constantly told Elvis that he was different, special—and he grew up shy and rather a loner. Music became his escape and since his family could not afford lessons he taught himself to play the piano and learned the guitar from a family friend. He had a real ear for music and a very good memory, so he could play a song perfectly after hearing it just a couple of times.

Opposite: By the time Elvis was a teenager, the Presleys were living near Beale Street, Memphis, home of the blues. Elvis studied the way the black singers moved and dressed and began to develop his own personal style. Most teenagers at this time went for a neat, preppy look, but Elvis favored long, slicked-back hair and sideburns, and wore slick tailoring in strong colors. He purchased some of his favorite outfits from Lanskys, a tailor on Beale Street.

SUN STUDIO
FREE PARKING IN REAR
Sam Phillips
AVENUE
710
SUN
TOUR INFO.
OPEN
10 - 6PM
TOURS
DAILY...

Birth of rock 'n' roll

Right: An early portrait. At first Elvis wanted to become a gospel singer, but he also loved to play hillbilly music. By combining the two, with blues thrown into the mix as well, he developed his own sound that was quite unlike that of established singers at the time. This unique sound later became known as rockabilly, and then as rock 'n' roll.

Opposite: In 1953 Elvis recorded a song at Sun Records in Memphis, a studio owned by Sam Phillips and Marion Keisker. Nothing came of it immediately and Elvis continued with his regular job as a truck driver. However, Sam Phillips called him back a while later and set him rehearsing with two much more experienced musicians, Scotty Moore and Bill Black. The three of them recorded a blues number, "That's Alright, Mama" and soon afterward a local disk jockey, Dewey Phillips, played the record around 14 times in one evening on his "Red Hot and Blue" show. Thousands of phone calls followed, and to everyone's surprise the music seemed to appeal equally to both black and white audiences. Phillips later explained what he found unique about Elvis, "He sings Negro songs with a white voice which borrows in mood and emphasis from the country style, modified by popular music. It's a blend of them all."

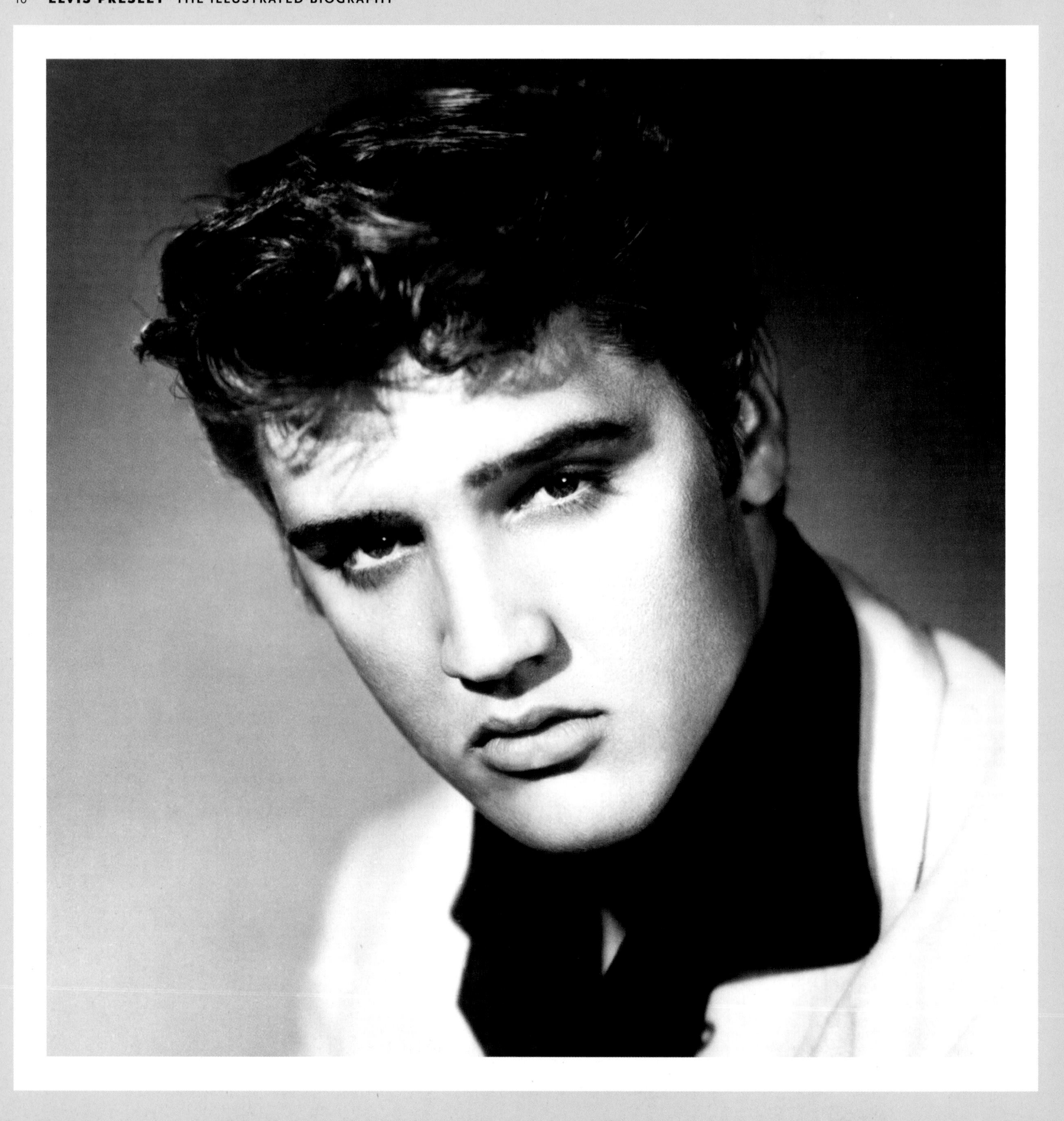

1954: Elvis and the Blue Moon Boys

Opposite: Despite his new-found success as a singer, Elvis continued to drive a truck for Crown Electric during the day until November 1954. At first Elvis and the Blue Moon Boys were managed by Scotty Moore, but later DJ Bob Neal took over, organizing bookings and concert tours and advertising Elvis as "the freshest, newest voice in country music." Since Elvis was still underage, his management contract with Neal was signed by Vernon and Gladys on his behalf.

Right: Elvis always sang with great emotion. The group began to play regularly at the Eagle's Nest in Memphis, but soon Neal got them a booking at Nashville's Grand Ole Opry. This most famous venue for country singing had never before featured an unknown singer, so they were all overjoyed. Unfortunately their new style of music was not received well by the Opry audience, who were more used to traditional country singers. Elvis was even advised to stick to driving trucks by the Opry's talent coordinator, Jim Denny. Fortunately he did not take the advice; but he would never play the Opry again.

Success at the Louisiana Hayride

Left: The Louisiana Hayride was broadcast on KWKH from the Municipal Auditorium in Shreveport. Elvis and the Blue Moon Boys first appeared here on October 16, 1954, and were and soon signed a contract to appear weekly on a Saturday night.

Opposite: An early informal photograph of Elvis. By the end of 1954 the boys were touring almost full time. They often appeared in one venue, then drove all night to appear somewhere else, with only a few hours sleep in the back of the car. Elvis coped with the demands of their schedule well, rarely tiring—although he could sleep for hours when the opportunity came. There was already an established fan club, founded by Marion Keisker of Sun Records, and many fans came to watch Elvis and the Blue Moon Boys wherever they appeared.

The Colonel steps in

Opposite: Guitarist Scotty Moore with Elvis. Bill Black, the other member of the Blue Moon Boys, played bass and later DJ Fontana, whom they met at the Louisiana Hayride, joined them as drummer. Although by the end of 1954 the boys were famous locally, still mainly on the Country music circuit, they had still not achieved national recognition—but it was not to be long in coming. In October 1954 they were brought to the attention of Colonel Tom Parker, a showbusiness promoter who was famous for his business acumen.

Above: Colonel Tom Parker with Elvis. Although his title was only an honorary one—conferred by a state governor—the Colonel insisted on using it at all times. He had started his career in carnival, but after becoming manager of singer Eddy Arnold he had become involved in showbusiness. After noticing the overheated audience reaction to Elvis the Colonel realized he was onto something special, and soon began moves to take over. He started by getting bookings farther afield.

Girls, girls, and more girls

Above and opposite: In May 1955, Elvis and his band began a three-week tour with Hank Snow's All-Star Jamboree. During a concert in Jacksonville, Florida, female fans went wild as he swiveled his hips and shook his legs—most singers of the time hardly moved as they performed. Many girls jumped onto the stage, trying to grab Elvis and tear his clothes off. Police guards were knocked to the ground in the rush and fans also attempted to break into his dressing room. Soon such behavior was a regular occurrence and Elvis loved it. He may have had a reputation for being quiet and polite—but he also loved women and was never known to turn a good-looking one away. Although he had a steady girlfriend—his high-school sweetheart, Dixie Locke—he also dated several other women regularly, including June Juanico, whom he met at a concert in Biloxi, Mississippi, late that June. Dixie broke up with Elvis at the end of that year, not because of the other women, but because he no longer had any spare time to spend with her. As well as continual concert tours he was also performing regularly on radio and recording new singles for release.

Baby, Let's Play House

Right: Elvis released "Baby, Let's Play House"/"I'm Left, You're Right, She's Gone" in April 1955. The A side appeared to refer to pre-marital sex and was roundly condemned by some, but by July the record had made it into the *Billboard* Top Ten. It was the first Elvis record to make it into the charts, but was soon followed by "I Forgot to Remember To Forget"/"Mystery Train," which stayed in the *Billboard* Top Ten for 40 weeks.

Opposite: Elvis himself could not understand the fuss about his stage presence; he danced on stage and sang the way he did because he had grown up alongside gospel singers and the blues singers of Beale Street—he didn't think of himself as a rebel, it was just his natural way. Elvis was to say "Rhythm is something you either have or don't have, but when you have it, you have it all over." The Colonel, however, recognized that Elvis reached a new, untapped audience—repressed teenagers who were rebelling against authority—and that the new rock 'n' roll music expressed how they were feeling.

November 1955: RCA signs up Elvis

Opposite: Elvis had given the Colonel the right to manage his career in August 1955, although he was still under contract to Bob Neal for another year. Atlantic Records bid $25,000 for Elvis, but were turned down. In November, after extensive negotiation by Colonel Parker, RCA bought Elvis's contract from Sam Phillips for $35,000. Elvis himself received $5,000, which he used to buy a car.

Above: Around this time Elvis began to develop his style to reach a wider audience, moving away from rockabilly and into rock 'n' roll. His style continued to evolve gradually throughout his career; sometimes existing fans did not approve, but he always picked up new ones. Some consider that the Colonel was manipulating the changes for profit, but a developing maturity and changes in presentation are part of any true artist's career.

Checking in at the Heartbreak Hotel

Left: Elvis in the recording studio, backed by gospel quartet the Jordanaires: Gordon Stoker, Neal Matthews, Jr., Hoyt Hawkins, and Hugh Jarrett. At the beginning of 1956 he had recorded his first single for RCA, "Heartbreak Hotel." Despite the fears of RCA executives, the single quickly proved to be a massive hit, reaching No.1 in the *Billboard* Pop Chart as well as No. 1 in the *Billboard* Country Chart.

Opposite: Early in 1956 Colonel Parker founded Presley Music Inc. to publish all the songs that Elvis recorded. The new company established a 50/50 partnership with Hill & Range Music for five years. By mid-1956, Elvis was bringing in half of RCA's income.

Jamming with the Dorsey Brothers

Opposite: On March 13, 1956, the first album, *Elvis Presley*, was released by RCA, who had already been swamped with 362,000 advance orders. The LP stayed in the *Billboard* extended-play album chart for a total of 68 weeks and went on to sell over a million copies, becoming Elvis's first Gold album. It was not only the album that was doing so well, though—RCA's Top 25 Best Sellers List included an amazing total of six Elvis singles.

Above: Between January 28 and March 24, 1956 Elvis made six appearances on *Stage Show*, the CBS program produced by Jackie Gleeson and starring Tommy and Jimmy Dorsey. It was the first time that he had reached a wider national audience, and his popularity rose quite sharply as a result.

Hollywood, here I come

Opposite: Despite the outstanding success of Elvis's career so far, the Colonel was already planning for the future. At the beginning of April 1956 he arranged for Elvis to take a screen test in Hollywood, which led to a seven-year movie contract with Paramount Pictures. Elvis greatly admired dramatic actors, such as James Dean and Marlon Brando, and he hoped that he would be able to follow in their footsteps.

Left: Elvis takes a turn at the drums. He was a self-taught musician and could learn quickly.

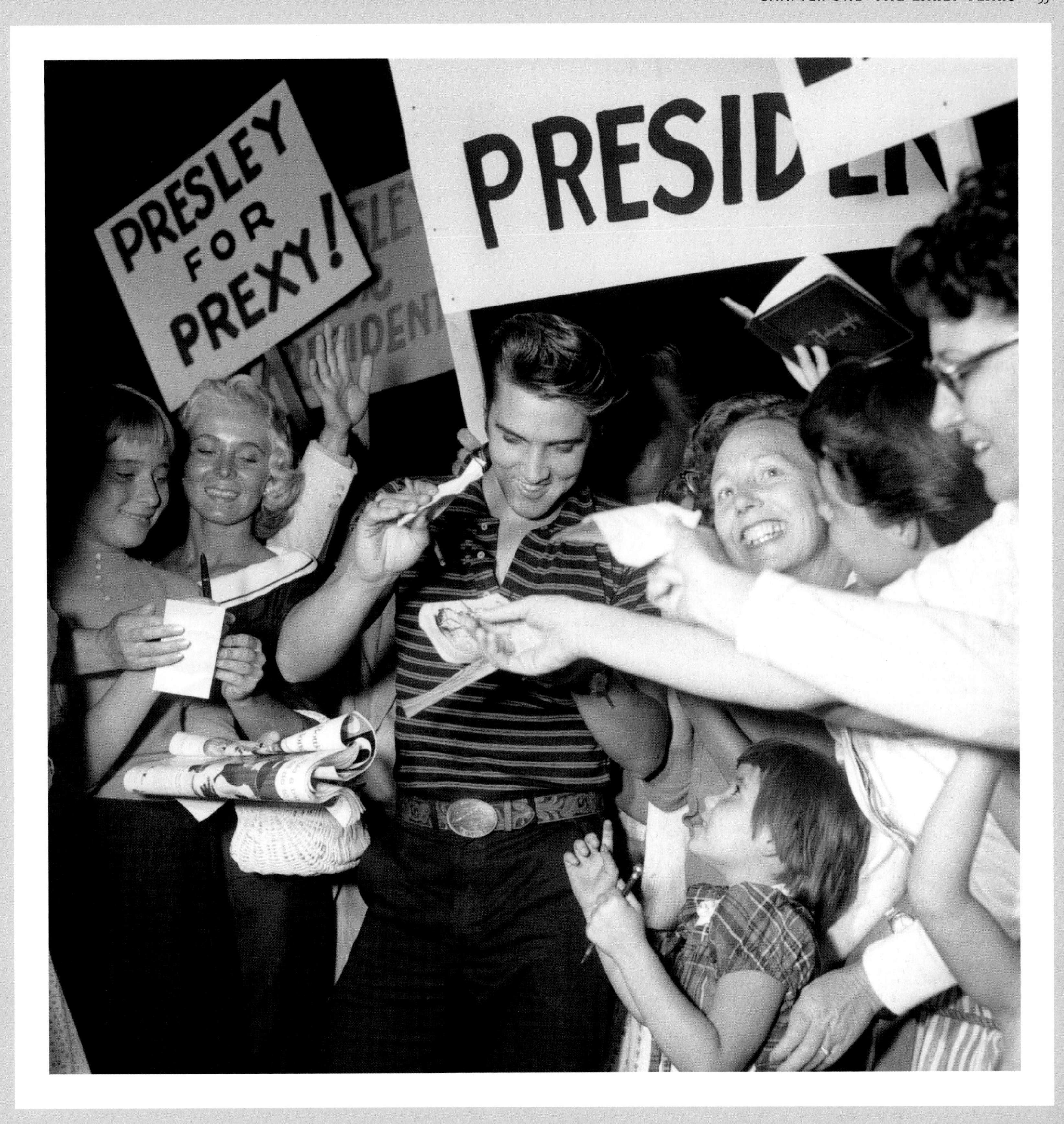
PRESLEY
FOR
PREXY!

All in a day's work

Above: Elvis signs autographs for a few lucky fans in Nashville, Tennessee—he had been recording in the nearby studios. His schedule in this period was packed full of concerts, interviews, and recording sessions—he was working hard to make the most of his sudden success. Wherever he was in the country he also had to make it back to Shreveport each Saturday night to appear on the *Louisiana Hayride*—his contract with them did not run out until December 1956.

Opposite: It was rumored that at the start of Elvis's career the Colonel had paid girls to scream at his concerts—but it certainly wasn't necessary by this time, if it had ever been. As well as being an exciting and talented performer, Elvis was very handsome and knew instinctively how to charm everyone around him.

RCA VICTOR

Heartbreak Hotel hits gold

Opposite: Elvis receives his first Gold record, after "Heartbreak Hotel" sells a million copies. The song was written by Mae Axton and Tommy Durdon, and Elvis had heard it for the first time at a disk jockey convention in November 1955. He quickly decided that he wanted to record it, and had acquired the rights to do so. The writers had originally been inspired by a newspaper article about a young man who had committed suicide.

Above: Elvis signs autographs for a group of young fans. Due to the demands of his career, coupled with the increasing problem of having to deal with hysterical fans whenever he went out, Elvis's movements were becoming more and more restricted. He was already at least one step removed from "normal" life, and was beginning to lay down the foundations for the lifestyle that was ultimately to lead to his downfall.

Love 'em and leave 'em

Opposite: Elvis leans toward teenage girls who are trying to reach him on stage. He had a natural stage presence and loved to tease the audience—which was usually made up mostly of young girls. Their jealous boyfriends were sometimes a problem, however, and in some towns in Texas Elvis needed protection from the police. In November 1956 Louis Balint, an unemployed steelworker, was fined after attacking Elvis because he believed his wife's passion for the singer had caused their marriage to fail.

Right: A scheduled four-week run at the New Frontier Hotel in Las Vegas in April 1956 was not a success—the middle-aged audience expected a more sedate style, from established entertainers such as Frank Sinatra. The raunchiness of Elvis and the raw power of rock 'n' roll came as a shock and the series of concerts continued only for two weeks.

MUSIC

June 1956: Appearing with Milton Berle

Opposite: Elvis appeared twice on *The Milton Berle Show* in 1956: the first program was in January, broadcast from the deck of the USS *Hancock*, moored in San Diego Naval Station; the second in June. The first show had an unusual location, but the second had far more impact—it was the first time Elvis sang his new single, "Hound Dog," on television. The audience appeared to love the song and their reaction encouraged Elvis to new heights.

Above: As Elvis reached the final part of "Hound Dog" the tempo slowed down and he began to thrust his hips in time to music. It was distinctively suggestive, and the studio audience went wild, both. That night, *Milton Berle* outdid *Sergeant Bilko* in the ratings. However, the next morning critics condemned Elvis's performance, calling it "primitive," "vulgar," and "tinged with... animalism."

You ain't nothing but a hound dog

Above: When Elvis appeared on *The Steve Allen Show* the following month—which was scheduled against Ed Sullivan—he was asked to moderate his performance. He appeared in rather a bad sketch, then donned a tuxedo and sang "Hound Dog" to a basset hound. Elvis wasn't happy about it, but he agreed to do it. Many of Elvis's fans were also not amused and they demonstrated outside NBC Studios the following morning.

Opposite: In August 1956, Elvis appeared twice at the Florida Theater in Jacksonville, and juvenile court judge Marion Gooding attended the first concert to see what all the fuss was about. After watching Elvis wriggle and shake as he sang, the judge asked that the show be toned down. For the second concert, Elvis only wriggled his little finger!

New wheels

Left: The first car Elvis owned was a 1942 Lincoln Zephyr coupé, which his parents bought him for his 18th birthday. In January 1956 RCA bought him a brand new convertible, but fans often defaced it by writing their names and phone numbers across the paintwork. In later years Elvis gave cars to many of his friends. He was always generous, saying, "Money's meant to be spread around. The more happiness it helps create, the more it's worth."

Opposite: Elvis was still constantly criticized publicly—some people did not like his music, the way he moved, the way he dressed, or his hairstyle. In person, Elvis could almost always win over his detractors when they encountered his good manners and charming personality. The Colonel loved all the controversy—it was all publicity, and publicity led to more sales. He was constantly coming up with new ideas to keep the fans happy and to promote "his boy."

Highs and lows of success

Opposite: Elvis poses with his favorite guitar, a Gibson J200. He was given the instrument by Gibson in 1956 after Scotty Moore signed an endorsement deal with the company. Perhaps they hoped Elvis would endorse their brand too, but the Colonel would not allow it. However, Elvis used this guitar for many concerts and appeared with it in several of his early movies. After he returned from the army in 1960 the guitar was totally refurbished, and he continued to play it into the 1970s.

Above: Elvis with his parents. Gladys had always told Elvis he was special—but now that he was, she didn't like it. She was upset by the crowds of young women who constantly swarmed around him and by the lack of privacy in their personal lives. Elvis had provided her with considerable emotional support for many years, but now he was always away touring. Mother and son were still close—but he did not have nearly as much time to spend with her as he had in the past.

August 1956: Love Me Tender

Opposite and above: Elvis on set during filming of his first movie, *Love Me Tender*, with costars Richard Egan and Debra Paget. Although Elvis had a three-picture contract with Paramount, they initially had no suitable vehicle for him so they loaned him out to Twentieth Century Fox for this Civil War drama. Elvis played Clint Reno, the youngest son of a farming family, who stays behind when his brothers go to war. After the eldest brother, Vance (Richard Egan), is presumed dead, his girlfriend, Cathy (Debra Paget), marries Clint instead. When Vance returns the family is torn apart, and at the end Clint is killed in a shoot-out. In case fans hated a movie in which Elvis was killed, an alternative ending was filmed in which Clint lives—but in the released version Elvis just appears again to sing over the closing credits. This is the only Elvis movie that was not written specifically for him and critical reviews for his performance were rather mixed, but director David Weisbart—who had directed James Dean in *Rebel Without a Cause*—thought he had great natural ability. The movie was originally entitled *The Reno Brothers*, but after Elvis had a massive hit with one of the featured songs, "Love Me Tender," the movie title was altered to match.

Recording the soundtrack

Left and opposite: Elvis looks relaxed during the recording of the soundtrack for *Love Me Tender* in August 1956. The music for the title song was based on the Civil War ballad "Aura Lee" with a new lyric written by Ken Darby. The movie included a further three songs: "Let Me," "We're Gonna Move," and "Poor Boy." There was not enough material for an LP, so RCA released them on a 45rpm EP instead. Elvis's usual backing band, comprising Scotty Moore, Bill Black, and D.J. Fontana, was replaced on the soundtrack EP by the Ken Darby Trio.

Highest ratings in television history

Above: Ed Sullivan with Elvis during rehearsals for an appearance on the show. The Colonel had approached Sullivan about featuring Elvis earlier, but had been firmly turned down, However, once Sullivan saw what Elvis did to the ratings he backed down and booked him for three appearances—at a fee of $50,000, which was rather more than the Colonel had originally asked for, and triple Sullivan's previous highest fee. The first show was hosted by Charles Laughton, as Sullivan was recuperating from a car accident: it received the highest ratings in television history.

Opposite: The Colonel chats to Ed Sullivan, as Elvis looks on. His second appearance on *The Ed Sullivan Show* featured a performance of the song "Love Me Tender," which resulted in advance orders of two million copies—and luckily the Colonel had been canny enough to retain publishing rights to the movie's score.

Homecoming at Tupelo

Opposite: In September 1956, Elvis's birthplace, Tupelo, inaugurated Elvis Presley Day. Main Street had a banner saying "Tupelo Welcomes Elvis Presley Home" and there was a big parade in his honor. The Colonel refused to allow Elvis to ride in the parade because of security problems, but he did perform at a homecoming concert. He wore a blue velvet shirt, which Natalie Wood had made for him. There were rumors they were having an affair, but in fact they were just good friends.

Above: Colonel Parker always had plenty of photographs of Elvis for fans to buy, and Elvis always patiently signed them. The past few months had increased his stage confidence and he played the crowd at Tupelo, coming to the edge of the stage and leaning down so the fans could just reach the ends of his fingers. Vernon and Gladys were part of the celebration, but Gladys later said that she had felt very uncomfortable, because they had been really poor when they lived in Tupelo.

Breaking records

Left: In 1956 Elvis released two LPs: *Elvis* and *Elvis Presley*, both of which went to Gold. He also released four classic singles, all of which went to Platinum—some of them more than once: "Heartbreak Hotel"/"I was the One;" "Hound Dog"/"Don't Be Cruel"; "Love Me Tender"; "I Want You, I Need You, I Love You."

Opposite: Elvis with his Martin D-28 guitar, which he used regularly from 1955 to 1956. Elvis bought the Martin secondhand from a store in Memphis and used it for most of his performances and recordings until he was given the Gibson J200. The Martin has a custom-made tooled leather cover, with the name "Elvis Presley" stamped cross the front—Elvis had labeled his previous guitars with stick-on lettering.

ELVIS

November 1956: Elvis and Liberace

Opposite: By the time Elvis appeared on *The Ed Sullivan Show* for the third time, he had earned the nickname "Elvis the Pelvis" and Sullivan had become concerned for his "family show" image. To avoid problems Sullivan decided to crop Elvis—and he was filmed only from the waist up. It has been estimated that at least one of the three Sullivan performances was seen by 52 million people: one out of every three Americans at the time.

Above: Elvis had first met Liberace in Las Vegas when they were both appearing there in April 1956 and they became close friends. Elvis always sent flowers to Liberace's opening nights. In November 1956 Elvis was in the audience at Liberace's concert at the Riviera Hotel, and afterward they exchanged jackets and posed for photographs. Liberace's gold jacket became the inspiration for the famous gold lamé suit made for Elvis by Nudie Cohen in 1957.

The Million Dollar Quartet

Opposite: The Million Dollar Quartet: Jerry Lee Lewis, Carl Perkins, Elvis Presley, and Johnny Cash come together for a late night jam session at Sun Studios in December 1956. All four singers were signed up to Sam Phillips' Sun Studios label, although he had sold Elvis's contract on to RCA at Colonel Parker's instigation a year earlier. With his wider exposure Elvis was already riding high: *Billboard* had recently designated "Heartbreak Hotel" their No. 1 single for 1956.

Above: *Love Me Tender* was released in November 1956, and entered *Variety*'s National Box Office Survey at No. 2. The Colonel already had come to understand that Elvis-related merchandise would be a winner and he had started companies to sell items such as jeans, charm bracelets, hair pomade, and bubblegum cards.

Chapter Two

In The Army

Home, sweet home

Opposite: As soon as Elvis had sufficient money he bought a new house for his parents and himself. It was situated in Audubon Drive, in a quiet residential area of Memphis—but as Elvis became even more famous, fans began to hang around outside in their hundreds. This was not only intruding on the Presleys' lives but was also extremely annoying for their neighbors. Elvis decided that they needed a home with more privacy, so Vernon and Gladys began to look around for one.

Right: Graceland, a Georgian colonial-style mansion, had been built in 1939 for Dr. Thomas Moore and his wife, on land that had been owned by Mrs Moore's great-aunt Grace—hence the name. It was built well back from Highway 51—later renamed Elvis Presley Boulevard—and stood in 13.75 acres of land, so was very secluded. Vernon and Gladys fell in love with the house at once, and Elvis was also enthusiastic when he saw it and bought it at once for $102,500, well outbidding a rival offer of $35,000 from the YMCA. Gladys was really happy to move in, planning her own chicken coop and hog pen, but she soon began to feel very isolated. In town, she had been part of a social circle of casual get-togethers, but now she was away from all her friends. Elvis was always away touring, and when he was at home she had very little time with him as Graceland had also become home to many members of his permanent entourage, as well as a floating population of hangers-on.

Loving You

Left: Meanwhile Elvis had completed his second movie, *Loving You*, for Paramount, with Dolores Hart and Lizabeth Scott. The storyline was based on his own life—an unknown singer with a new sound, who is initially labeled a bad influence but turns out to be a fine young man. Elvis's hair was dyed black for the part of Deke Rivers and it suited him well—he was naturally a dark blond, but he kept it black for the rest of his life. A single from the movie, "Teddy Bear"/"Loving You," was the first to be distributed in the UK, where it quickly sold over a million copies.

Opposite: By the start of 1957, Elvis could not step into the street without gathering a crowd around him. Armed security guards were on hand whenever he went out and he was constantly surrounded by a group of men who acted as his friends and as a support group. Members of this entourage were on hand 24 hours a day to entertain Elvis but also keep an eye on his general safety, since he often walked in his sleep when he was worried or upset. The entourage were often badly behaved and they soon earned the nickname of the "Memphis Mafia."

GOLDWYN-MAYER

February 1957: Jailhouse Rock

Opposite: Elvis with actress Barbara Lang and fans, outside MGM studios in Hollywood, just before starting work on *Jailhouse Rock*. Barbara was originally named to star opposite Elvis in the movie, but in the end the part went to Judy Tyler instead. During this period Elvis had a regular girlfriend, former beauty queen Anita Wood, but although they were together for several years this did not stop him from dating other women.

Right: A still from *Jailhouse Rock*, which was a low-budget movie shot in black-and-white with stylized sets. The storyline played on Elvis's bad boy image—but in the end his rather surly and unpleasant character gets his comeuppance and reforms, so all ends happily. The simplistic film style suited the rather serious subject matter and *Jailhouse Rock* is widely regarded as Elvis's best movie.

Dance fever

Opposite: *Jailhouse Rock* is most famous for an exciting dance sequence in which Elvis sings the title track, backed by professional dancers as inmates in a jail cellblock. Elvis had initially been unsure about the idea, but choreographer Alex Romero created a routine based on how the singer moved naturally on stage, so he felt comfortable and became more enthusiastic. Elvis got on well with professional dancer Russ Tamblyn, who coached him to develop his dancing style.

Above: Elvis performs on the set of *Jailhouse Rock* with Bill Black (bass), D.J. Fontana (drums), co-star Judy Tyler, songwriter Mike Stoller (piano), and Scotty Moore (guitar). Judy had just married so she and Elvis were not romantically involved, but they became great friends. Elvis was devastated when she and her husband were killed in a car accident a soon after shooting was finished, and he could not bear to attend the movie's premiere.

Your Country Needs You!

Left: Elvis had recently received notification to attend a pre-induction physical to see if he was eligible for draft. The news that the famous ducktail and sideburns would soon be shorn off into a standard army short-back-and-sides made the front page of *Billboard*, and caused panic amongst the loyal fans.

Opposite: Elvis took the physical in February 1958 at the Kennedy Veterans Hospital in Memphis. He was accompanied to the hospital by Las Vegas dancer Dorothy Harmony, who had spent Christmas with the Presleys. Elvis was classed 1–A, and therefore would be called up—although the army said it was unlikely to be within the next six months.

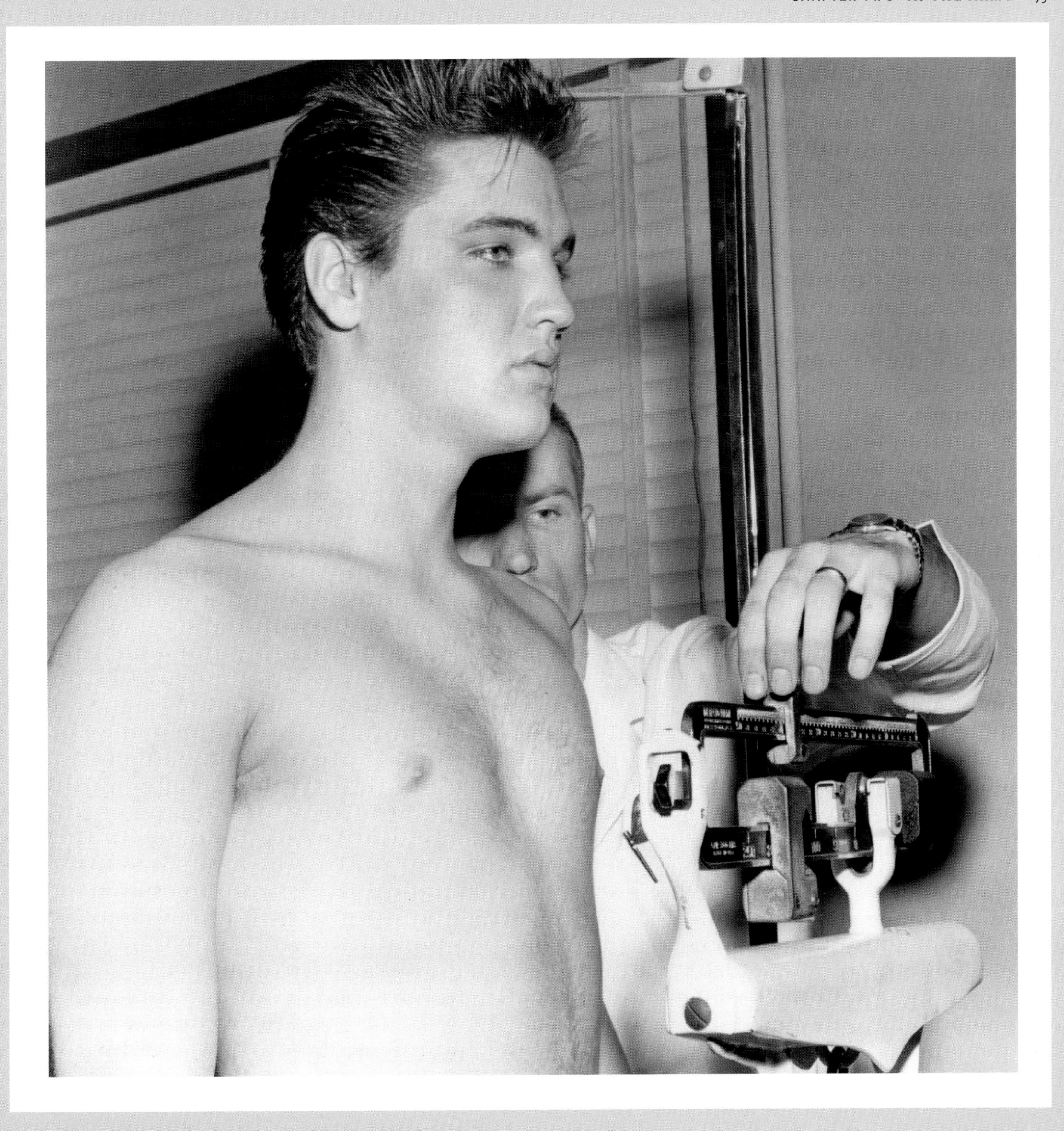

March 1958: King Creole

Left: In *King Creole*, Elvis gave his most critically-acclaimed performance as Danny Fisher, who comes up from the ghetto to seek fame and fortune as a singer in the New Orleans jazz clubs. Director Michael Curtiz had also been responsible for *Casablanca*; other film industry heavyweights on the production included Hall Wallis as producer and Russell Harlan as cinematographer. The cast included acclaimed actors such as Oscar-nominee Carolyn Jones, as well as a young Walter Matthau. The expertise and experience lavished on the movie certainly showed on the screen—unfortunately few of the later Presley movies had all the same benefits.

Opposite: Elvis fans were always eager for new pics of their star, and the Colonel always made sure there were plenty of movie stills available. While on location in New Orleans for *King Creole*, the crowds of excited Elvis fans were so large that tighter security was organized—for instance, the elevator in the hotel did not stop at the top floor, which was where all the cast and crew were staying. Elvis was disappointed that he could not try the legendary New Orleans' cuisine because of security concerns—instead, he had to be content with room service.

Proud to serve

Opposite: Although Elvis had been called up earlier, his draft was delayed by 60 days so he could finish filming *King Creole*—otherwise Paramount would have lost the thousands of dollars already spent in pre-production. Elvis arrived at the draft board early on March 24, and then he and the other recruits were taken to Kennedy Veterans Hospital for a final check-up.

Right: Elvis, along with the other recruits, is sworn in at the draft board in Memphis by Major Elbert P. Turner. Elvis had been offered special status by the military—the navy suggested he could spend his time entertaining troops, the army thought he would be better employed touring recruiting offices. He refused these offers and requested to be treated just like all the other recruits—he knew it would quickly cause resentment if he didn't do his duty properly. He told reporters he was proud to serve his country.

Parting is such sweet sorrow

Above: Girlfriend Anita Wood (front center) comforts Gladys as her son is taken away to begin his army career. Meanwhile the Colonel had covered all bases to keep "his boy" in the spotlight—Elvis had recorded a string of songs to be released in his absence. "All Shook Up," "Teddy Bear," and "Jailhouse Rock" had all reached the No.1 spot in 1957, and *King Creole* was due for release in July 1958—along with the soundtrack LP, which quickly raced into the *Billboard* Top Pop Album chart.

Opposite: Elvis heads off to Fort Chaffee in Arkansas, where he is to get his kit and be assigned for basic training. The bus taking him there was followed on the road by hundreds of private cars, and when it made a scheduled stop for refreshments there were already hundreds of people waiting. The crowd was so thick that none of the recruits could actually leave the bus for their coffee and sandwiches.

EATS-39
915
A
GROW
RECRUITER

March 25, 1958: the famous haircut

Left: The army barber takes Elvis back to basics, watched by 55 reporters and photographers. In all the commotion, Elvis forgot to pay the barber his 65 cent fee, and had to be called back. He had already been issued the sum of $7 in army pay, and told reporters that he planned to open a loan company with it.

Opposite: At Fort Chaffee, Elvis also had to sit through a two-hour talk on the rights and privileges of a private, as well as getting his jabs for typhoid, tetanus, and Asian flu. Although he refused to sign autographs while he was "in ranks," he dealt with all the media attention with his usual good humor. The military had decided to allow full media access to the whole process, in the hope that this would prevent any problems and soon lead to the press attention letting up. However, they soon realized they had vastly underestimated the media frenzy that would ensue—and they had failed to consider the hundreds of fans, all eager to catch a glimpse of their hero.

PRESLEY
U.S. ARMY
U.S. ARMY

Media circus

Opposite and right: Elvis made his bed, modeled his uniform, and generally posed for photographers at every opportunity. He was pictured having breakfast, being issued with his army fatigues and size 12 boots, and waiting around with the other recruits. It was soon announced that he and six other recruits were being assigned to the 2nd Armored Division, based at Fort Hood near Killeen in Texas. This was General Patton's "Hell on Wheels" outfit, and Elvis and the others would be there for eight weeks learning how to be soldiers. Since there was still no sign of a let-up in media attention, and after seeing what had happened at Fort Chaffee, the army had reconsidered their open-access policy. After Elvis arrived at Fort Hood they had decided to allow one day of media access—after which, Private Presley would become an ordinary soldier.

In training

Left: The trip from Fort Chaffee to Fort Hood was a day-long journey. To fool the fans and the press, the bus taking the recruits bypassed its usual stops, in Dallas and Waxahachie, and instead made an unscheduled stop in Hillsboro, Texas. Two of the largest recruits were detailed to sit on either side of Elvis and the group sat down for refreshments. It was 25 minutes before Elvis was recognized—but then pandemonium broke out. It took some time to get everyone back on the bus and away.

Opposite: After all the attention, Elvis settles down for a well-earned rest. This was the first time he had been away from his family without the support of his entourage, but after a few initial problems he soon settled. After a while the other soldiers accepted him as "one of the boys," and in some respects this was probably one of the most "normal" period of Elvis's entire life.

PRESLEY

August 1958: Hitting the heights and plumbing the depths

Opposite: If a soldier had family nearby he was able to move out to live off barracks, so Elvis soon rented a house near Fort Hood and Vernon and Gladys, Vernon's mother Minnie Presley, and one member of the Memphis Mafia, Lamar Pike, moved in to take care of him. Meanwhile his singing career was not at a standstill—"Hard Headed Woman" was released as a single in 1958 and by August it was certified gold by the RIAA.

Above: Gladys had been depressed and a secret drinker for some time, but in August 1958 the hot Texas weather brought her health problems to a head. She returned to Memphis to see a doctor—and was rushed into hospital. Elvis had compassionate leave to visit her bedside, but two days later she died. Elvis was inconsolable, and could not stop stroking her body and calling for her to come back. At her funeral he was supported by friends, but just over a week later he had to return to Fort Hood.

U.S. ARMY

On maneuvers

Opposite: Elvis on maneuvers in Germany. He arrived by ship in Bremerhaven and was transferred by train to the US base at Friedberg, near Frankfurt. There he was assigned to Company C, which had been chosen because it was the company that spent the most time away on maneuvers—and thus away from public attention. Elvis drove a jeep for Reconnaissance Platoon Sergeant Ira Jones and according to Jones, Elvis "scrubbed, washed and greased" the jeep too.

Above: After buying a second-hand BMW 507 sports car, Elvis agreed to pose for publicity pictures with a model who had been hired to hand over the keys. His entourage had also come with him to Germany, so he bought his father an old Cadillac and a Volkswagen for the selection of Memphis Mafia members in attendance. Lamar Pike was usually responsible for driving Elvis from the house they had rented to the base, where Elvis began his duties at 7.00 a.m.

PRESLEY

Entertaining the troops

Opposite: Elvis entertains his fellow soldiers. Although in many ways his days in the army were good for Elvis, they did introduce him to one thing that were to prove a destructive influence in the future: amphetamines. He had been begun taking them to stay awake during night maneuvers, but was soon taking them daily—both to keep going and to stay slim. A diet of junk food was still his preference, but up until now he had expended enough energy on stage to keep his weight in check. Now it was beginning to catch up with him.

Above: Bill Haley with Elvis. Haley and the Comets appeared in Frankfurt on October 23, 1958 and afterwards in Stuttgart. Elvis went to see both performances, but had to remain backstage for fear of causing pandemonium amongst the audience. Since he had enough money to go away whenever he had some leave, Elvis also often took his entourage off to Paris, where they partied with showgirls from the Folies Bergère, the Lido, and the Moulin Rouge.

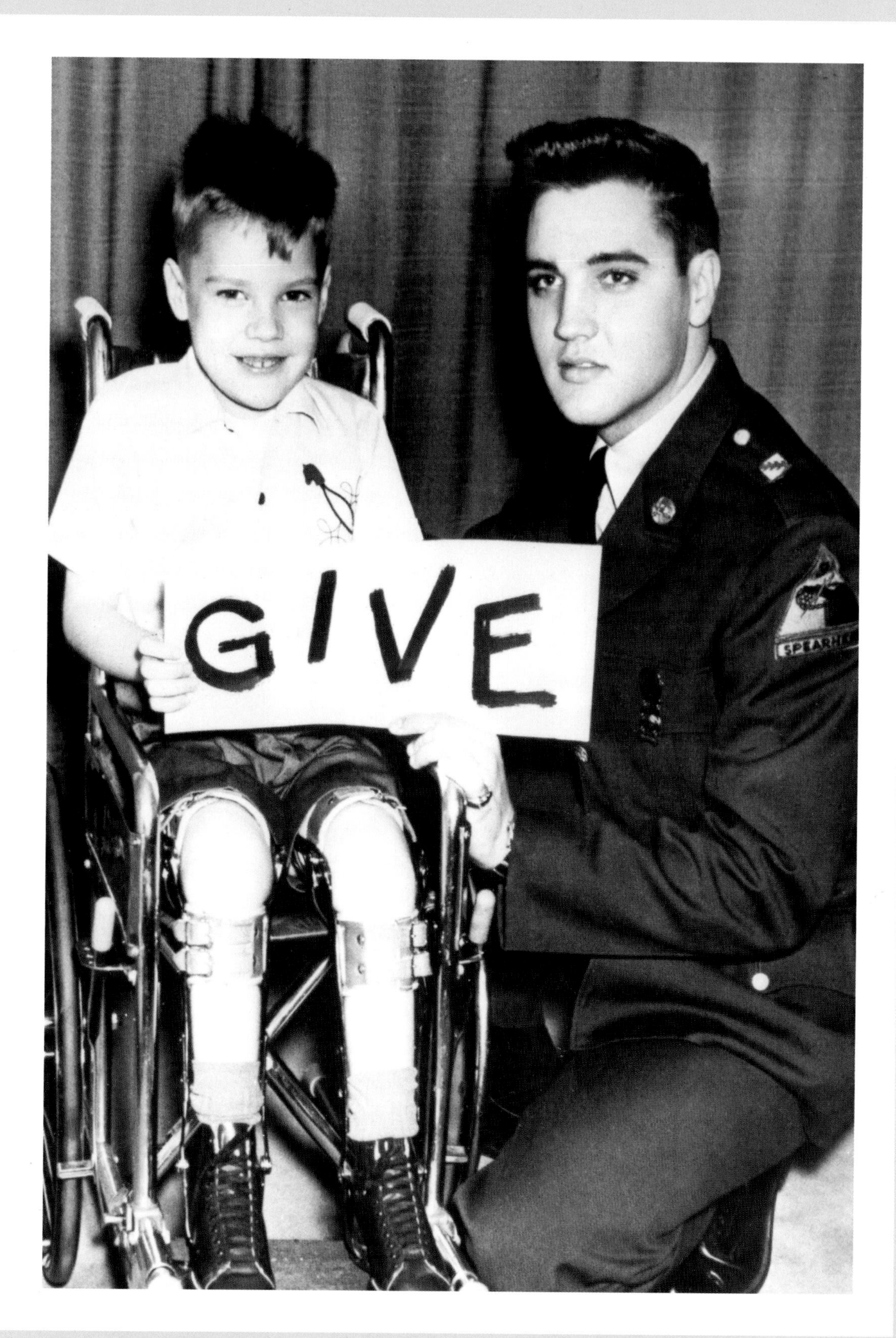

1959 March of Dimes

Opposite: In all the time that Elvis was in the Army, he never appeared in an organized concert or sang for a real audience. This was partly because he did not want to encourage others to see him differently, and partly because the Colonel had instructed him not to. Back in the USA, the canny promoter was using "his boy's" absence and the lack of material to negotiate hard with RCA and with several Hollywood studios.

Right: Charity appeals were a different matter. Elvis posed with Robert Stephen Marquette, the polio-stricken son of a master sergeant in the army, and one of the resulting photographs taken then became a 1959 March of Dimes poster.

U.S. ARMY
3
SPEARHEAD

November 1959: Priscilla

Right: In November 1959, Elvis was introduced to fourteen-year-old Priscilla Beaulieu, step-daughter of air force officer Paul Beaulieu. They got on very well, and that Christmas he took her to local festivities and met her parents. His friendship with Priscilla was kept very private—until she arrived at the airport to wave goodbye when Elvis finally left Germany to return to civilian life in the USA in March 1960. He promised to call her, but she assumed that she would never see him again.

Opposite: During his army career Elvis was promoted twice. In January 1960, just before his discharge, Elvis rose to the rank of sergeant and was in command of a a three-man reconnaissance team.

March 1960: Back home for good

Opposite: Elvis at a press conference after he arrived back in the USA. He told reporters that he wanted to rest—but in fact the Colonel already had a busy schedule planned. There was not only a recording session lined up, but also an appearance on the *Frank Sinatra Show*, as well as a new movie ready to go. Ever mindful of the details, the Colonel had also made sure there were plenty of fans on hand to wave and shout, proving that Elvis was still on top, despite his two-year absence from the spotlight.

Above: The Colonel welcomes "his boy" home. When Elvis was given his severance pay, the Colonel jokingly requested his percentage in commission—so Elvis laughed and handed him the entire envelope containing $109.54.

A new direction

Opposite: Elvis on the set of *G.I. Blues* for Paramount, his first movie for two years. A musical comedy, with a storyline that was heavily based on Elvis's army career, the picture was aimed squarely at a more mature audience than previous Elvis productions. His character in the movie was in a tank division serving in Germany—but all footage featuring Elvis was shot in Hollywood. In April, 1960 just before filming began, Elvis also recorded two of his classic hits: "Are You Lonesome Tonight?" and "It's Now or Never."

Right: Elvis's first appearance following his discharge was to be on the fourth of Frank Sinatra's Timex Special TV shows, for which Sinatra had offered to pay Elvis $125,000. Throughout the train journey to Miami, where Elvis was to record his appearance program, the track was lined with fans and press. His performance on the show was a surprise to the fans though—he was a polished professional, elegantly dressed in a tuxedo. Elvis sang three solo songs with aplomb, then joined Sinatra, harmonizing while Sinatra sang "Love Me Tender." A few fans mourned the passing of a rock 'n' roll star— but most welcomed the new maturity in style.

Chapter Three

The Hollywood Years

August 1960: Flaming Star

Opposite and right: Two stills from *Flaming Star*, the serious movie that Elvis had been wanting to make for some time. His character, Pacer Burton, was the offspring of a white settler and a Kiowa Indian woman, and the plot dealt with the prejudice he experiences as a person of mixed race and what happens when an Indian uprising forces him to take sides. Director Don Siegal was well-respected and the reviews were complimentary, but the score contained only two songs and the fans were disappointed. The movie did not do as well at the box office as some other Elvis pictures—so it was soon back to the lightweight material again. Elvis still sports quite short hair at this time—he did not now grow it as long as it had been before his army days.

November 1960: Wild in the Country

Above: Elvis embarked on his third movie that year, *Wild in the Country*, which was also for Twentieth-Century Fox, only a month after shooting finished on *Flaming Star*. This was another serious movie, with quite a dark plot, but after it was noted that *Flaming Star* was not performing as well as expected at the box office, several songs were quickly written into the story. Elvis had three leading ladies: Tuesday Weld, Hope Lange and Millie Perkins.

Opposite: Elvis and Tuesday Weld were very close and there were rumors that they would marry. In fact he was still seeing Anita Wood, amongst others—but had also stayed in touch with Priscilla in Germany. He hoped to persuade her parents to allow her to come to America to see him, but she was still only 15 and understandably they were reluctant—although they liked Elvis and considered him to be a nice boy.

Blue Hawaii

Left: *Blue Hawaii*, which began filming in March 1961 on location in Hawaii, was the most successful movie commercially of Elvis's career. A light and amusing story, with more songs than ever before, the picture also made great use of the stunning Hawaiian scenery. The success of *Blue Hawaii* sealed Elvis' fate as far as his film career was concerned. Although *Flaming Star* and *Wild in the Country* had not lost money, neither had they done as well as Elvis movies were expected to. The Colonel used the amazing box-office success of *Blue Hawaii* to convince Elvis that his fans preferred him in lightweight musical comedies. When asked about his career in an interview, Elvis said, "I've had intellectuals tell me that I've got to progress as an actor...I'd like to progress, but I'm smart enough to realize that you can't bite off more than you can chew in this racket."

Opposite: Elvis serenades his love interest in *Blue Hawaii*, Maile, who was played by Joan Blackman. Juliet Prowse, who had recently appeared with Elvis in *G.I. Blues*, was originally to have appeared in this movie too, but at the last minute she was replaced by the lesser-known actress.

Leading lady

Left: Elvis with his co-star, Joan Blackman, in *Blue Hawaii*. He usually got on very well with his leading ladies, his natural charm and personality quickly winning them over. Whenever a new picture began shooting, there here were soon rumors that Elvis had begun an affair with whoever was playing opposite him, but these were rarely true. Many times the stories were invented by the publicity department to make sure interest was building in the movie even before it was released. In fact while he was shooting *Blue Hawaii*, Elvis was still seeing Anita Wood regulary and was also trying to persuade Priscilla's parents to allow her to come to America.

Opposite: Elvis at a Halloween party with actress Joan Blackshaw.

November 1961: Kid Galahad

Opposite: Elvis was coached for the boxing scenes in *Kid Galahad* by Mushy Callahan, a world champion junior welterweight boxer. *Kid Galahad* was Elvis's third movie in 1961—he had only recently finished *Follow That Dream*, also for United Artists. For his role as a boxer in *Kid Galahad*, Elvis began training before the start of production by doing road work, going on a strict protein diet, punching bags, and sparring for hours with professionals. He lost 12 pounds in the process.

Right: This still from *Girls! Girls! Girls!*, which began filming in April 1962, caused an outrage when it was released to publicize the film—many felt that the pose was rather indecent. The soundtrack of *Girls! Girls! Girls!* features one of Elvis's classic songs, "Return to Sender," although it was not originally written for the movie. Instead the Colonel heard it elsewhere and realized it would be perfect for Elvis. The single of "Return to Sender" was released in October 1962 and went on to sell more than 14 million copies. After Elvis died and the United States postal service issued a stamp to commemorate his memory, many Americans wrote false addresses on letters with the Elvis stamp so the envelope would be returned marked "Return to Sender"—thus making the stamp more valuable.

Girls! Girls! Girls!

Left: The screenplay of *Girls! Girls! Girls!* included lots of songs—Elvis was now being presented as an entertainer rather than an actor. The director was Norman Taurog, and again Hall Wallis produced.

Opposite: In 1961, Elvis only appeared live in concert three times, twice in Memphis and once at a charity event on behalf of the USS *Arizona*, moored at Pearl Harbor, Hawaii. Live appearances now presented too much of a security risk—the fans still went wild whenever Elvis appeared, so he had to enter and leave the auditorium in secret. When he was on stage fans threw themselves forward to try to reach him, and there was a distinct danger that someone would soon be badly hurt. For the rest of the 1960s, Elvis concentrated on his movie career instead—but since he was now making as many as three pictures a year the schedules were becoming very short.

September 1962: At the World's Fair in Seattle

Left: Elvis in a still from *It Happened at the World's Fair*, made for MGM. Filming was on location in Seattle, where there was indeed a major fair in progress, called the Seattle Century 21 Exposition. The wardrobe that was specially made for Elvis to wear in the movie cost $9,300 and included ten suits, two cashmere coats, four sport coats, 15 pairs of slacks, 30 shirts and 55 ties.

Opposite: At the fair, Elvis's character, Mike Edwards, meets and falls for nurse Diane Warren, portrayed by Joan O'Brien. In real life Elvis was still seeing Anita Wood—but after Priscilla Beaulieu appeared back on the scene at the end of 1962 Anita soon realized it was time to move on.

January 1963: Fun in Acapulco

Opposite: Elvis checks the view through the camera. Filming on *Fun in Acapulco* began early in the New Year, after Elvis had spent Christmas with Priscilla at Graceland, the first time they had been together since he left Germany in 1960. Elvis had been trying to persuade her parents to let her come to America since then, and finally they had relented. Officially she was staying with friends—she was still not yet 17—and the visit was kept very quiet as everyone was aware of the negative publicity that could follow if Elvis's involvement with such a young girl got out.

Above: Elvis with Ursula Andress in *Fun in Acapulco*. Although the exteriors were shot on location in Mexico, Elvis stayed on Paramount's Hollywood lot for all his filming. After the success of Priscilla's visit, he persuaded her parents to allow her to finish her education in America. Officially Priscilla lived with Vernon and his new wife, Dee Stanley, and attended the Immaculate Conception High School, but after she graduated she began to spend increasing amounts of time with Elvis at Graceland.

Priscilla moves in

Opposite: Since Elvis was now away in Hollywood filming for much of the year Priscilla soon moved into Graceland permanently, although she was still never seen in public with Elvis. When he was able to take time out from his busy filming schedule to come home they spent all their time together, but even then they were not alone. Assorted members of the Memphis Mafia were always present, along with various wives and girlfriends—mostly much older than Priscilla—and she was shy and constantly afraid of putting a foot wrong.

Right: By this time Elvis had completed 14 movies, most of which had been outstanding box office successes, and all of which had made money. Producer Hall Wallis once commented, "An Elvis Presley picture is the only sure thing in Hollywood." Elvis was no longer performing live, but his music was still in the charts: the soundtrack for *G.I. Blues* was No. 1 in the *Billboard* Top 100 album chart for 10 weeks and remained in the chart for 111 weeks. The album from *Blue Hawaii* was No. 1 for 20 weeks and appeared in the chart for 79 weeks.

July 1963: Viva Las Vegas

Opposite and right: In July of that year Elvis started work on his 15th movie, *Viva Las Vegas*. His co-star was Swedish actress and singer Ann-Margret and Elvis found that for once his partner could match his singing and dancing skills. In addition, the two stars quickly realized that they were kindred spirits, both full of energy and mischief. Ann-Margret was not intimidated by the Memphis Mafia and soon came to be regarded as "one of the boys." Although rumors of an affair with his co-star were a routine way of generating publicity for the forthcoming movie, in this instance many people commented that they had never seen Elvis as relaxed and happy as he was with Ann-Margret. Unfortunately it was not to last. When Ann-Margret went to London to promote her previous movie, the press reported that she had spoken of marrying Elvis. Priscilla was deeply upset, and Elvis quickly told the reporters that the story was untrue and that if he intended to marry they would hear about it from him. Ann-Margret later denied having said anything but she and Elvis did eventually drift apart—although they remained friends for the rest of his life and he always sent flowers to her on opening nights.

IRCUS

March 1964: Elvis joins the circus

Opposite: Elvis strums his guitar in a publicity still from *Roustabout*, his 16th film and the 7th for Paramount. The month before filming started The Beatles had arrived in America for the first time, receiving a reception that rivaled the public response to Elvis in hysteria and intensity. The group had already taken Britain and Europe by storm, and their first US hit record was storming up the charts. Despite the threat of competition, Elvis sent the Fab Four a congratulatory telegram. The Beatles wanted to meet up, but it was not to happen for another year.

Above: In *Roustabout*, Elvis was paired with experienced actress Barbara Stanwyck. Initially the two had a few problems, but by the end of filming Elvis commented that she had inspired him to improve his acting skills. Unfortunately he had already realized that he was never going to be taken seriously as an actor: on the day filming started producer Hall Wallis was widely reported as commenting that his artistic and critically acclaimed films such as *Becket* could only be funded because of the profits from lightweight Elvis movies.

Entertainer of the Year

Left: Elvis gets to grips with some serious painting, with a little help from a friend, in a movie still from the mid-1960s. At the end of 1964 he was voted sixth top box office draw by theater owners, and was presented with an award as Tennessee's Entertainer of the Year.

Opposite: A studio portrait of Elvis dating from the mid-1960s. In 1964 he purchased the U.S.S. *Potomac*, which had once been owned by President Franklin D. Roosevelt and had been used as a "floating White House" during the Second World War. It had been moored as a tourist attraction at Long Beach, but Elvis planned to present it to the March of Dimes charity. However, when the charity realized how much the yacht would cost in upkeep, it turned the offer down. The yacht was finally accepted by the St. Jude Hospital in Memphis, a center that researched childhood diseases.

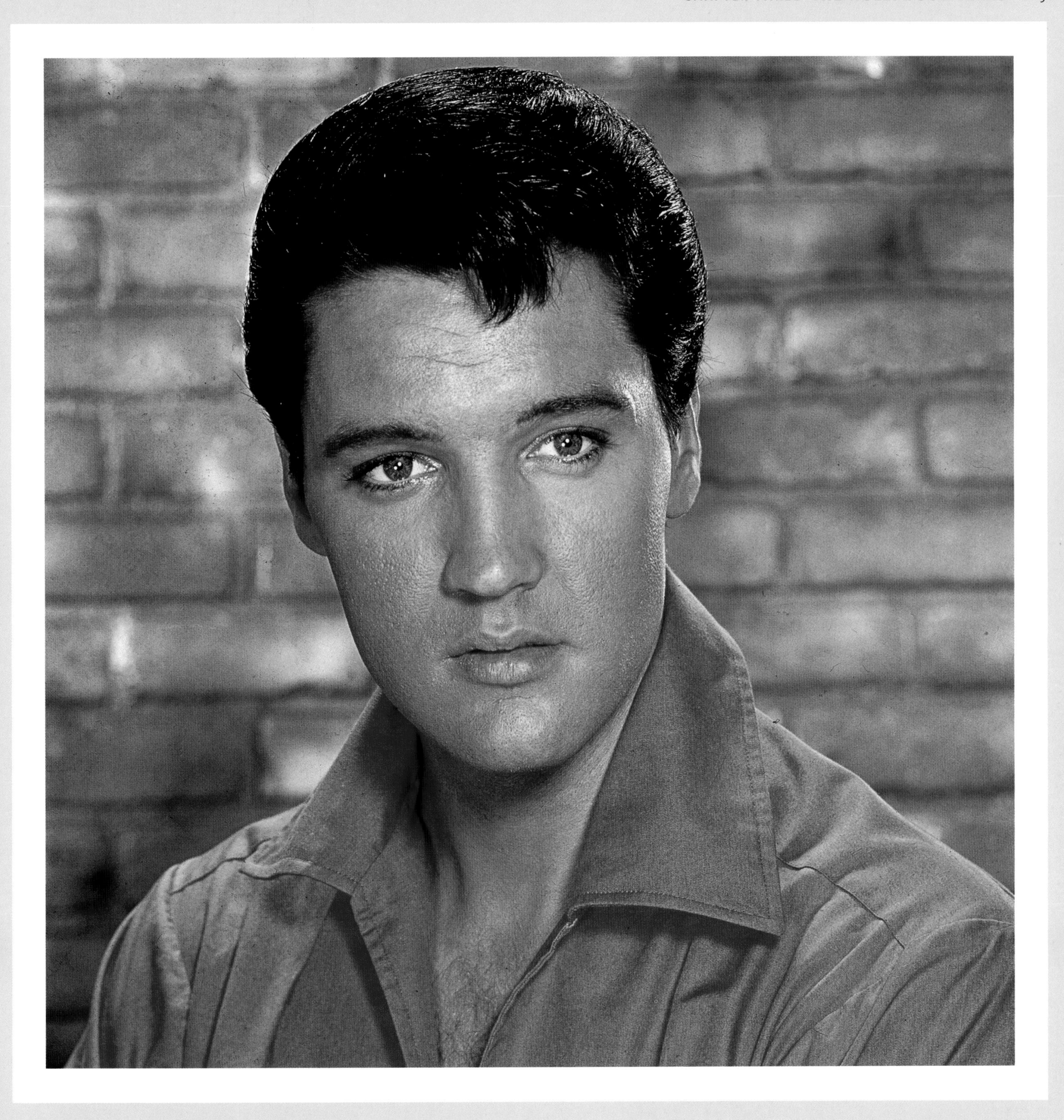

A tried and tested formula

Opposite: This still has all the elements of a typical Elvis movie of the mid-1960s: lots of girls, beautiful location and Elvis singing. Privately he was not only becoming bored with the formulaic plot lines but also with the poor quality of the songs that were being offered to him. Some of them were so bad that even the Colonel could see they were not suitable. However, much of the problem was as a result of an arrangement the Colonel himself had set up at the beginning, in which a songwriter had to forgo a part of the writer's royalty before Elvis would record a song. This meant that the best material was now no longer offered to Elvis. Things came to a head on *Girl Happy* in 1965, when Elvis walked out of the studio rather than finish recording. The following film, *Tickle Me*, had no original soundtrack—instead previously recorded songs were used.

Right: Elvis in *Harum Scarum*, a low budget movie that reused the sets from Cecil B. DeMille's 1925 picture *King of Kings* and costumes from the 1944 and 1955 versions of the movie *Kismet*. The shooting schedule lasted a mere 18 days.

May 1965: Frankie and Johnny

Opposite and above: In *Frankie and Johnny*, a lighthearted musical based on the folk song, "Frankie and Johnny," Elvis played a riverboat entertainer, which allowed scope for lots of songs—and Elvis looked dashing in period costume. His co-star was Donna Douglas, who later became famous as Elly May Clampett in the long running TV series *The Beverly Hillbillies*. The cast also included Robert Strauss, seen above with Elvis, who had appeared in a previous Elvis movie: *Girls! Girls! Girls!* as Sam, the owner of the Pirate's Den.

When *Frankie and Johnny* was released in March 1966 it did not do very well at the box office—although only by Elvis terms; it did not actually lose money—and the soundtrack album could only make it up to No. 20 in the charts. The record side was not doing that either: of all the singles released in 1965, only a gospel song, "Crying in the Chapel" made it into the *Billboard* Top 10, peaking at No. 3. The song had originally been recorded for *His Hand in Mine*, Elvis's first gospel LP, but was released as a single instead.

A return to the islands

Left and opposite: Elvis in *Paradise, Hawaiian Style*, which began filming in August 1965 and was released in July 1966. He was ill for part of the time during the making of the film, missing several days of pre-production recording and at one point going absent from the set. While on Hawaii, Elvis spent a lot of time at the Polynesian Cultural Center, which was the location for the "Drums of the Islands" production number. Along with his father, Vernon Presley, and Colonel Tom Parker, he also visited the U.S.S. *Arizona* Memorial, which his benefit concert in 1961 had helped to build. The three men laid a bell-shaped wreath with 1,177 carnations—one for each serviceman lost in December 1941 during the attack on Pearl Harbor. A few days after production moved back to the studio, on August 27, 1965, The Beatles finally met up with Elvis at his Bel Air home. Only a small group of family and friends were on hand for this historic meeting, which resulted in an impromptu jam session.

Paradise lost

Left: Elvis made three movies set in Hawaii: *Blue Hawaii*, which was outstandingly successful, *Girls! Girls! Girls*, which also did very well, and *Paradise, Hawaiian Style*. Most people would agree that *Paradise, Hawaiian Style* was not one of Elvis's best pictures—although it still went on to gross $2.5 million within six months of its release. However, Elvis had now lost his initial enthusiasm for making movies after realizing that he would never be respected as a serious actor.

Opposite: A promotional portrait of Elvis dating from the mid-1960s. *Paradise, Hawaiian Style* was quickly followed in early 1966 by *Spinout*, which was released nationwide the following November. The next two movies, *Easy Come, Easy Go* and *Double Trouble*, were already in production and had finished filming before *Spinout* was released. In fact Elvis only had a week off between finishing *Double Trouble* and starting on *Easy Come, Easy Go*.

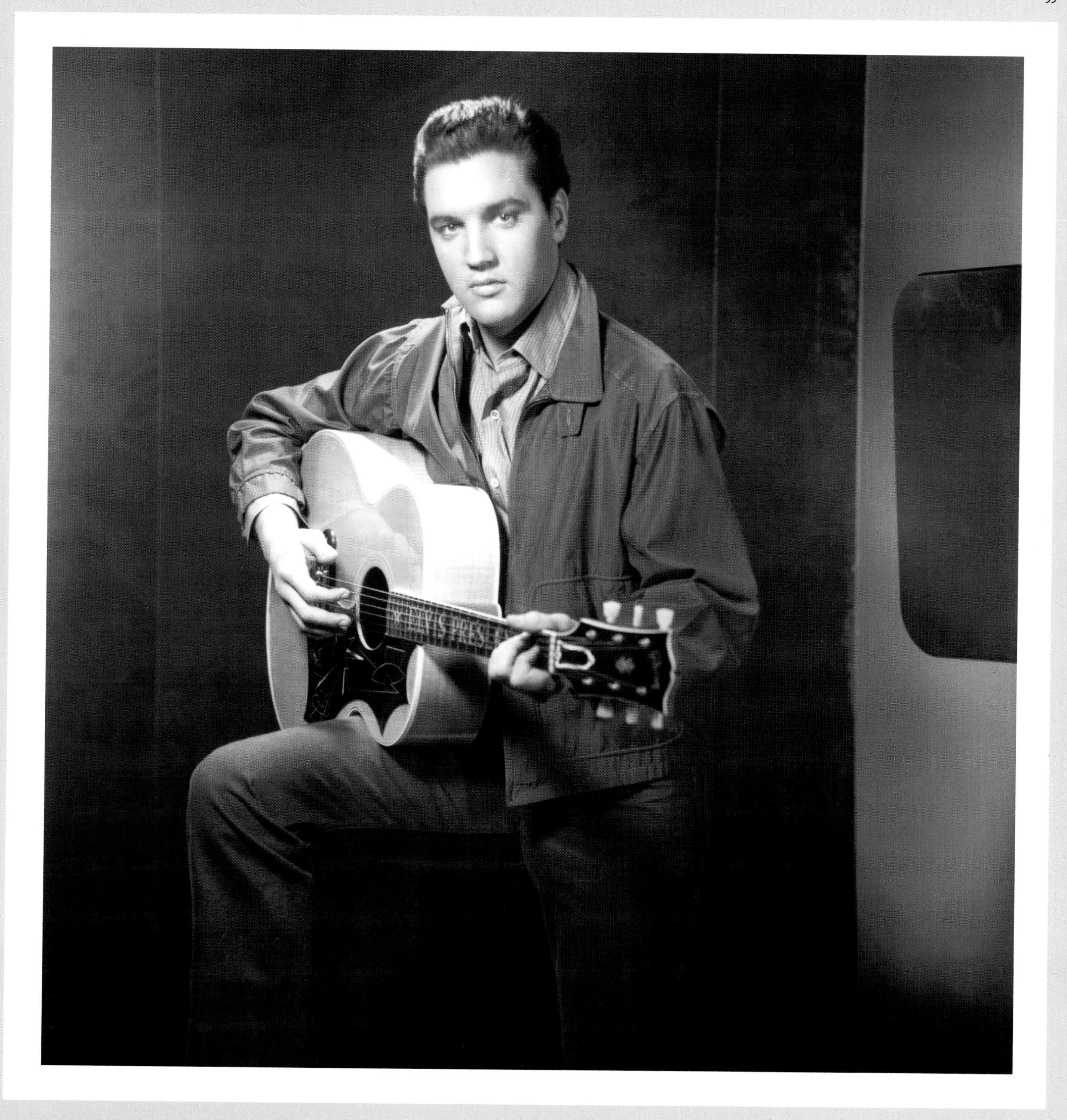

Colonel Parker and "his boy"

Opposite: A relaxed and smiling Elvis on set. It is not clear why he did not insist on better scripts—but perhaps, as in the past, he was content to rely on the Colonel's judgment. As long as the promises the Colonel made him were kept, Elvis went where he was told to go and did what he had to. However, he did protest about the quality of the songs.

Right: Colonel Tom Parker in the mid-1960s. No one will ever know exactly how much Elvis made during his lifetime—Elvis did not even know himself—and no one knows exactly how much the Colonel took for himself. The contracts certainly gave Elvis's manager a large share of the takings. He and his wife had a reputation for never spending their own money—they lived in Palm Springs in a house provided by the William Morris Agency and almost everyone found themselves contributing to the running expenses of the Colonel's office and staff.

Time to propose

Left: By the end of 1966, both the Colonel and Priscilla's parents were pressing Elvis to make up his mind about Priscilla. To persuade her parents to allow her to come to America in the first place, Elvis had apparently promised that they would marry when she was older. She had now been living at Graceland for nearly three years, and everyone felt that it was time he honored his commitment. Finally the Colonel told Elvis that either he married Priscilla or she would have to move out, so just before Christmas 1966 Elvis proposed.

Opposite: In early 1967 Elvis purchased a ranch in Wallis, Mississippi. He had first bought a horse for Priscilla, then horses for himself and all the members of the entourage, and soon the paddocks and barns at Graceland could no longer hold all the horses and equipment. Everything was quickly moved out to the Flying Circle G ranch—the G in its name stood for Graceland—and Elvis began spending increasing amounts of time there playing cowboys with his companions.

No break in filming

Opposite and above: Elvis in *Clambake*, with Will Hutchins and Shelley Fabares. Although Elvis now wanted to give up making movies, he still had contractual obligations, so the punishing production schedule continued. The Colonel was aware of Elvis's dissatisfaction and was making an effort to get the studios to improve his scripts and provide much better songs, but no one really wanted to tamper with what had previously been a winning formula. Elvis was totally uninterested in making *Clambake* and it was hard to get him to leave his ranch and report for work. Depressed, and reluctant to make yet another lightweight musical comedy, he put on a lot of weight during pre-production, which United Artists demanded he shed before the cameras could roll. Just before shooting was due to begin, Elvis slipped and hit his head, causing a concussion, so the schedule was delayed for more than two weeks. Although Elvis and the Memphis Mafia often played crazy stunts on set, on *Clambake* they were so out of control the studio was forced to protest.

May 1, 1967: Wedding day

Opposite and above: Elvis and Priscilla are married in a private ceremony in a room at the Aladdin Hotel in Las Vegas, by the Nevada Supreme Court Judge David Zenoff. Fourteen people were present at the ceremony, including Priscilla's parents and sister, Vernon and the Colonel. Only two members of the Memphis Mafia were invited to attend—much to the annoyance of many of the others—although they were all invited to the reception afterwards. Lack of space was given as the reason—but perhaps Priscilla just wanted, for once, to do something without the constant and often intrusive presence of the entourage. A press conference was held in the Aladdin Room of the hotel immediately after the eight-minute ceremony, and Priscilla faced the cameras for the first time at her husband's side, showing off her three-carat diamond ring for the cameras. When asked why it had taken him so long to get married, Elvis replied "I decided it would be best if I waited till I really knew for sure. And now I'm really sure."

Cutting the cake

Right: Priscilla and Elvis cut the six-tiered wedding cake. There were over 100 people at the reception, enjoying a buffet meal which included suckling pig, Southern fried chicken, and oysters. The guests were entertained by a string quartet playing romantic music. However, the exclusion of the entourage from the ceremony itself caused lasting resentment, and instigated discontent among some of the members.

Opposite: The happy couple under a shower of rice. After returning briefly to their home in Palm Springs straight after the ceremony, they soon left for a month-long honeymoon at the Flying Circle G ranch. Although many members of the Memphis Mafia inevitably came along too, they tried to give the new couple a little privacy and there were no household staff at the ranch. At the end of the honeymoon everyone returned to Graceland for another ceremony for all of the friends, family and staff who had missed the Vegas wedding.

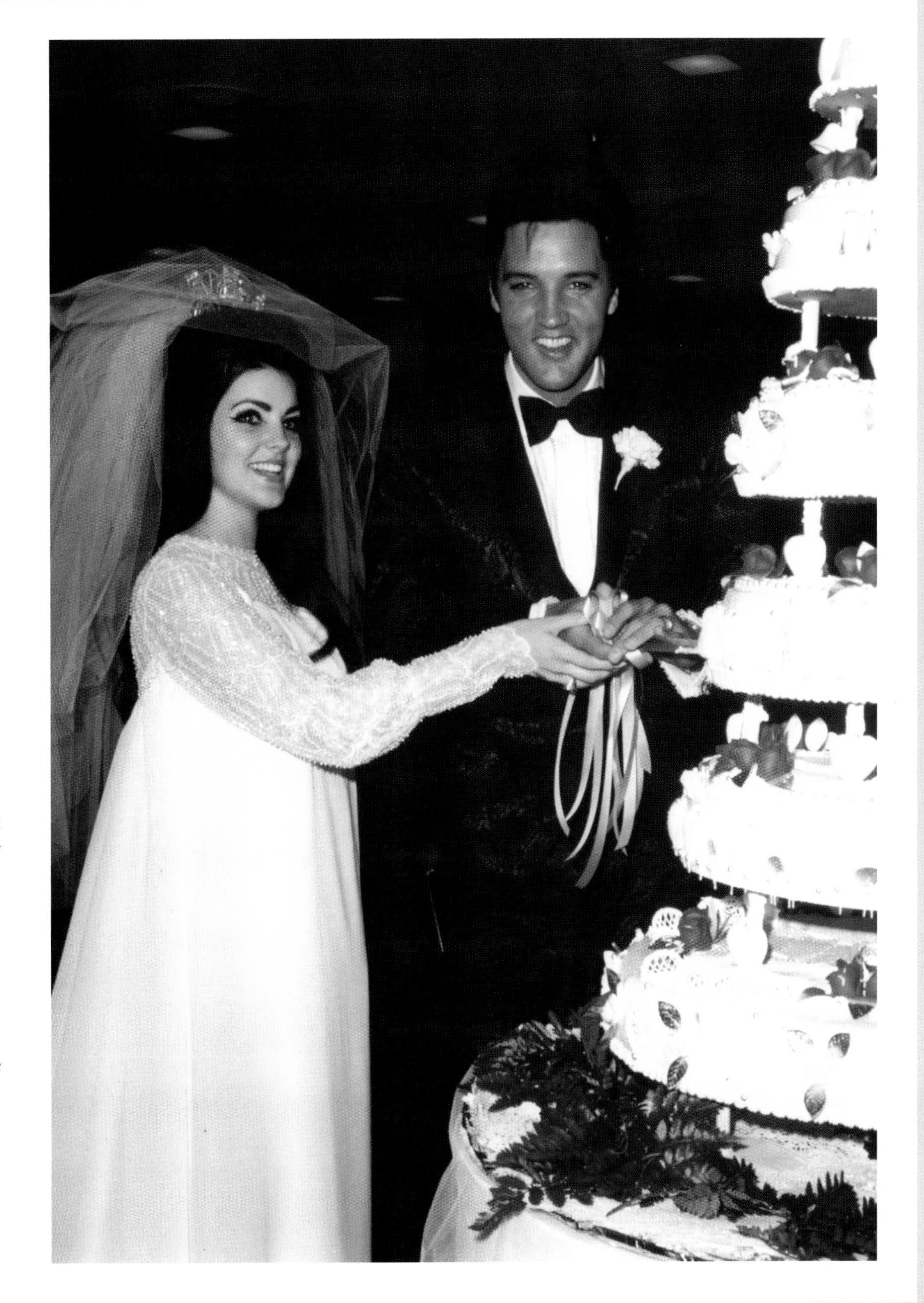

June 1967: Speedway

Opposite: In his movies, Elvis usually had an interesting job and was a man of action with an eye for the ladies. No matter how unlikely the scenario, he could also always find the opportunity for a song. He played both a racing driver and an airline pilot three times, as well as a photographer, a boxer, a navy frogman, a powerboat racer, and a doctor. He was also cast as a Native American Indian twice. During a press conference Elvis was asked what kind of scripts he liked. He replied, "Something with meaning. I couldn't dig always playing the the guy who'd get into a fight, beat the guy up, and in the next shot sing to him. However, as his career in Hollywood developed, he was rarely offered such scripts.

Left: Nancy Sinatra with Elvis in *Speedway*. The two stars had been romantically linked before Elvis's marriage, but again rumors began to circulate. However, when Priscilla was expecting Lisa Marie, it was Nancy who organized the baby shower.

Introducing Lisa Marie

Left: On February 1, 1968, exactly nine months after she and Elvis were married, Priscilla gave birth to a daughter weighing 6 lb15 oz. Elvis was overjoyed at the idea of becoming a father. At a press conference he told journalists that he was the "happiest man in the world."

Opposite: The happy family. Unfortunately, soon after Lisa Marie was born, Elvis made it clear to Priscilla that he was no longer physically attracted to her. Priscilla was left feeling unhappy and unfulfilled—and it would only be a matter of time before someone stepped in to comfort her.

The Welsh Elvis

Opposite and above: Elvis and Priscilla with Tom Jones in April 1968, after the Welsh singer's show at the Flamingo Hotel in Las Vegas. Like Elvis, Tom Jones generated a hysterical frenzy in his female fans when he performed—and they were often known to throw their underwear onto the stage. Elvis and Tom Jones had first met in 1965, and the Welshman later told reporters that listening to the early Elvis records had helped him to develop his style. By 1968 Elvis had not sung in front of a live audience for several years, but he confided that he wanted to make a comeback—and that he would really like to perform in Las Vegas. The advent of The Beatles had ushered in a popularity for groups and Elvis was concerned that perhaps solo singers were now seen as old-fashioned. However, seeing Tom Jones performing so successfully in Las Vegas convinced him otherwise—particularly as their singing styles were quite similar.

July 1968: Live a Little, Love a Little

Opposite: Elvis feeds a whale at Marineland in California. The whale had a starring role in *Live a Little, Love a Little*, appearing alongside actress Susan Henning in her role as a mermaid. A couple of months before this, at a karate tournament in Honolulu in May 1968, Elvis had met martial arts expert Mike Stone. Elvis had been interested in karate since being introduced to it during his time in the army. He suggested that Mike teach Priscilla karate—a decision he was to come to regret.

Right: Elvis with co-star Celeste Yarnall in *Live a Little, Love a Little*. In his role as a photographer he dates a model, played by Celeste, but his main love interest, Bernice, was played by Michelle Carey.

Time for a change

Left: Elvis and Colonel Parker on location during the filming of the last Presley movie, *Change of Habit*. By this time Elvis had decided that he wanted to return to singing and did not want to do any more movies. Ironically, the last few movies did have slightly more interesting plot lines and a somewhat better selection of songs—although they were still not the best of his career. *Charro!*, the 29th movie, which was released on March 13, 1969 was even a previously unheard of phenomenon: an Elvis movie with no songs. The only time Elvis was heard singing was on the title song played over the credits. In this movie he appeared rugged and handsome in a beard, which certainly pleased the fans.

Opposite: Elvis on set. Although some people believe that a great many of Elvis's movies were very poor, this is simply not true. In a career that spanned 31 films there were bound to be a few pictures that were not as good as others, and some are so much of their time that today they can appear rather kitsch. However, all the Elvis movies were financially successful and for a number of years he was one of Hollywood's top box office draws and one of its highest-paid actors. In a review of *Easy Come, Easy Go* in 1967, *Variety* said, "Anyone who has seen similar films recognizes the superior quality of Presley's films: the story makes sense; the songs are better, and better motivated; cast and direction are stronger; production values are first-rate."

M·G·M

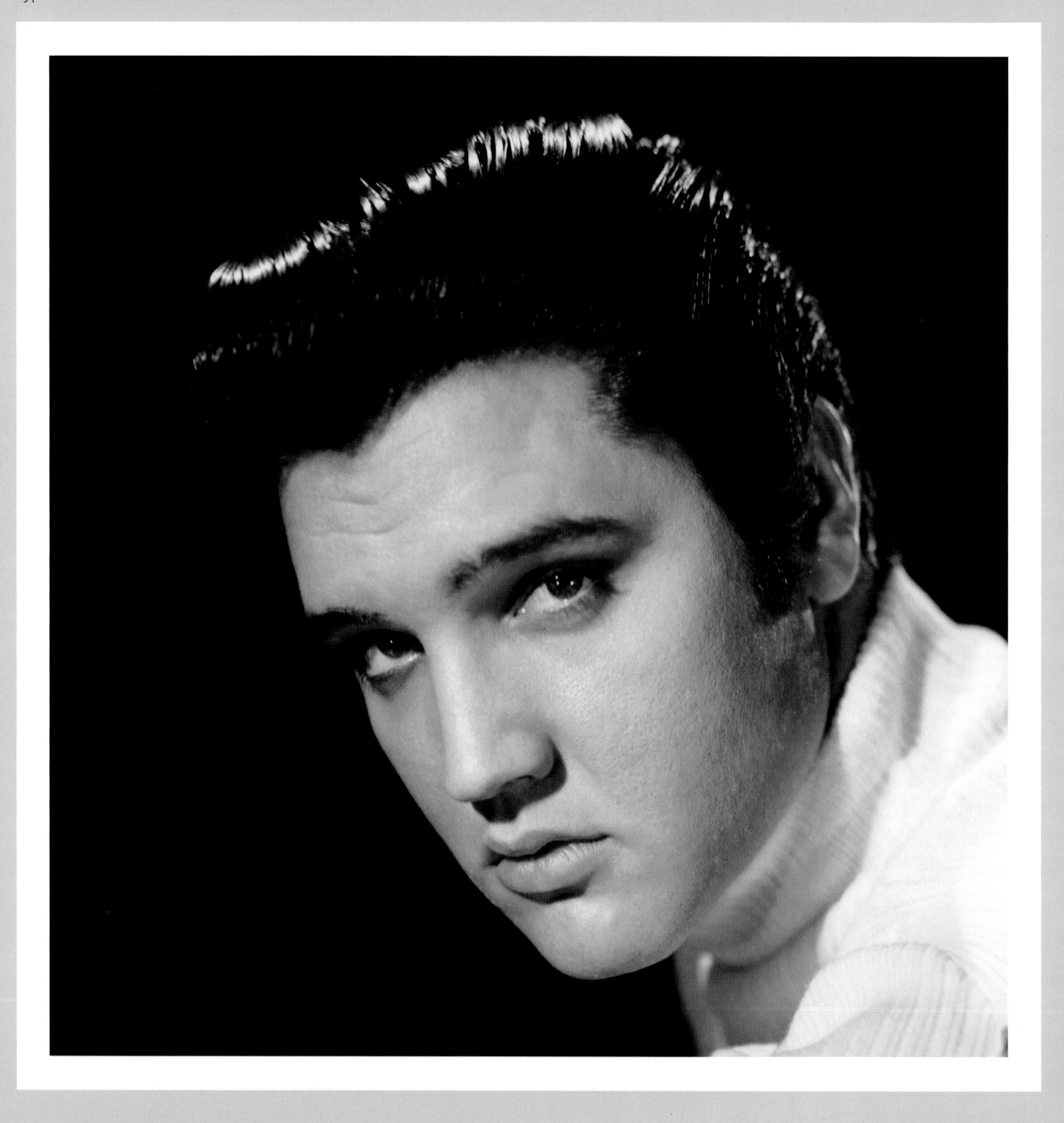

On the record

At the beginning of Elvis's movie career the film soundtracks usually had a selection of good songs especially written for him—although they also had to fit within the plot, however loosely. Eleven of the movie soundtrack albums went into the Top Ten, and of those, four went to No. 1. Some of the later movies were not so fortunate, and many of the songs selected were so poor that Elvis stormed out of the recording session in at least one instance. Two songs that he disliked in particular were "Song of the Shrimp" from *Girls! Girls! Girls!* and "Dominick" from *Stay Away, Joe*—which in the movie he had to sing to a prize bull. In fact he hated this last song so much that he made producer Felton Jarvis promise that "Dominick" would never appear on a record, even after his death. The last few pictures did have better songs—by then everyone had realized that better material was needed to get Elvis's career back on track. *Live a Little, Love a Little* even featured a future classic: "A Little Less Conversation," which became a hit single after it was remixed for a Nike promo in 2002.

Getting the Grammy

Opposite: Elvis once said that he knew practically every religious song that had ever been written. During his career he had some 105 Top 40 hits, many of which reached No, 1. He received 14 Grammy nominations from the National Academy of Recording Arts and Sciences (NARAS), but his three wins were all for gospel recordings. In 1967 the album *How Great Thou Art* was awarded Best Sacred Performance, in 1972 the album *He Touched Me* was awarded Best Inspirational Performance, and his live Memphis concert recording of the song "How Great Thou Art" was awarded Best Inspirational Performance Song.

Right: At the beginning of 1968, Elvis had announced that he would like to do a tour of Europe, but the plan never came off. In fact Elvis never toured out of America—except for three shows in Canada: Toronto in 1957, Ottawa on April 3, 1957 and Vancouver on August 31, 1957. Despite the triumphs to come in 1968, the year was sad for personal reasons: Elvis lost two old friends: Nick Adams, an actor he had met in Hollywood, and Dewey Phillips, the Memphis DJ who had first played Elvis's music on air.

Chapter Four

The Comeback

Preparing for a comeback

By mid 1968 it had been decided that Elvis would appear in a Christmas Special, to be broadcast on television by NBC—Elvis's first TV appearance for eight years. The program was recorded before a live audience in June 1968—the first time that Elvis had appeared live for seven years. The original plan proposed by the Colonel was that Elvis would just sing a selection of Christmas songs, but NBC wanted something a little more interesting, so producer Bob Finkel tried to convince Elvis to go for a more radical change of image. At first he was reluctant, but then director Steve Binder challenged him to walk down the street and see if he was recognized by any young people. It was many years since Elvis had been out in public without bodyguards, but he decided to give it a try. He and Steve Binder walked outside onto Sunset Boulevard alone and stood chatting on the street for several minutes. Not one person recognized Elvis, and afterwards he was much more relaxed and receptive to the new ideas being suggested.

Meeting old friends

When the *Comeback Special* was being recorded, Elvis met up with two members of his old backing group the Blue Moon Boys: guitarist Scotty Moore, and drummer D.J. Fontana. Unfortunately Bill Black, who had played bass, had died in 1965 during surgery to remove a brain tumor. In parts of the final show the three remaining members of the Blue Moon Boys sat together on stage in the round—along with several other friends and associates of Elvis—for an informal session of singing, jamming, and swapping stories. There were also set musical pieces, and sequences of Elvis taking the stage alone and performing many of his greatest rock 'n' roll hits and ballads, as well as introducing a new song, "Memories." The Colonel sat back until the program was very nearly complete—then demanded to know where the Christmas song was. Binder agreed to drop one in to the end of the show to avoid any argument—but later Elvis himself decided that a Christmas song just did not fit in with the rest of the material. The show finally closed with "If I Can Dream."

December 1968: The Comeback Special hits the screen

Above and opposite: Although it is usually referred to as *The '68 Special* or *The '68 Comeback Special*, the television program that revived Elvis's career was simply called *Elvis*. The Singer Company were sponsors of the show—although as makers of the famous sewing machine they had no obvious connection with either rock 'n' roll or Elvis. Director Steve Binder and his team decided to use the 60-minute slot to tell a story, so Chris Beard and Allan Blye wrote a script about a young man leaving home to search for happiness, the obstacles encountered along the way and the eventual journey back home. All the different segments related to music that Elvis had either recorded or that he liked. NBC was initially worried about the concept because featuring just one star in prime time was unheard of—normally there were also several guest stars. However, Elvis loved the whole idea and threw himself into the project with enthusiasm. Binder asked costume designer Bill Belew to design a range of outfits for Elvis to wear in the show, including the famous black leather suit with a high collar.

Guitar man

Opposite: Elvis and Susan Henning in the bordello scene, in which Elvis meets an innocent young girl who has just arrived to begin work as a "lady of the night." The two of them begin to get to know one another, then the bordello is raided and Elvis ends up out on the street and on his way again. The scene was completed, but when a representative from Singer saw it they demanded that it be removed because they felt it was too racy. The *Special* was initially broadcast in a version 60 minutes long, but the first cut was 90 minutes. After Elvis died a longer version was released, and this scene was replaced. Much of the unused *Special* footage was also packaged as *Elvis: One Night With You*.

Right: The opening scene featured Elvis and 89 guitar men in silhouette, echoing the famous cellblock sequence from *Jailhouse Rock*. The song "Guitar Man" was used as the theme link between the different segments of the story. The beautiful red Hagsrom guitar that Elvis plays in the opening scenes belonged to Al Casey, one of the experienced backing musicians on *The Comeback Special*. Elvis initially seemed nervous at performing a live concert after such a long absence, so Binder told him to think of it as a recording session, to which they would add pictures. When he first walked out onto the stage he was shaky, but as the audience responded to him an amazing surge of confidence brought back his natural instinct for performing.

Jamming the night away

Opposite: Elvis became so involved in the project that he began sleeping in his NBC dressing room. After rehearsals one night, Steve Binder came into the dressing room and found Elvis and his friends relaxing by jamming together, laughing and joking. He decided it would be great to add a laid-back sequence with a flavor of the real Elvis to the *Special*, and his first thought was to film it in the dressing room. This didn't prove practical, so the sequence became an informal gathering of Elvis and his friends—including Scotty Moore and D.J. Fontana—in front of a live audience. Invitation tickets were printed for the audience, but the Colonel insisted on having them all to distribute as he chose. Maybe this was his way of scuppering the idea, which he was never happy with, as on the very morning of filming Binder discovered the tickets had not been sent out. He and his associates quickly rounded up an audience via friends and family—even going down to the local hamburger restaurant to round up all the customers. As the sequence progressed Elvis forgot about the cameras, and in the event this was one of the most memorable sections of the *Special*.

Right: Belew designed a gold suit to symbolize success, in homage to the suit that Elvis had worn in 1957. Elvis refused to wear the full suit, but agreed to wear the gold jacket with a pair of black tuxedo pants.

If I can dream

Opposite: For the finale, Elvis sang standing in front of his name in lights. The show was originally supposed to end with him singing a Christmas song, but—as they got to know Elvis better and saw how deeply he was affected by the deaths of Robert Kennedy and Martin Luther King—Steve Binder was inspired to ask songwriter Earl Brown to write an inspirational song for the finale. That song would become the much loved "If I Can Dream," which was inspired by Martin Luther King's "I Have a Dream" speech. Elvis greatly admired King and had committed this speech to memory. The *Special* aired on December 3 and was seen by 42 percent of the viewing audience—making it the top show of the season and giving NBC its biggest ratings victory of the year.

Left: On June 26 there was a birthday party on set for Colonel Parker and Elvis sang a parody of "It Hurts Me" written for the occasion by Chris Beard and Allan Blye. The new version of the song began: "It hurts me to see the budget climb up to the sky..." and finished "...tell me the truth is it too much to ask for one lousy tired ol' Christmas song?"

INTERNATIONAL
BILL M LLER PRESENTS
ELVIS
SAMMY SHORE
THE IMPERIALS
SWEET INSPIRATIONS
BOBBY MORRIS ORCHESTRA
EXCITING
THE SKY-HIGH CROWN ROOM OPENS SOON
CASINO THEATRE
WAYNE COCHRAN
AND THE C.C. RIDERS
IKE AND TINA TURNER
REVUE
10 TH STORY WINDOW
COMING SOON
LAS VEGAS FIRST
LEGITIMATE
THEATRE

Comeback in Las Vegas

Opposite and above: After *The '68 Comeback Special* was transmitted, the *New York Times* told everyone that Elvis had found his way home. Fans both old and new rushed to buy his records, and Elvis announced that he wanted to return to singing. With Elvis back on top, the Colonel quickly organized a four-week booking at the International Hotel in Las Vegas, which was due to open in July 1969. Elvis was not the opening act for the hotel—that honor went to Barbara Streisand, because the Colonel felt that a first performer in a new venue would have to deal with all kinds of teething problems to do with the staging. However, it was still a bit of a gamble—Elvis's last appearance at Las Vegas had been a disaster, but he was now being expected to fill a venue that would have a capacity almost double that of others in Vegas. On the opening night Elvis was visibly nervous, but he soon got into his stride and his uninhibited enjoyment of singing soon won the audience over. The show was a sensational success, and the hotel quickly booked him to appear twice a year for the next five years.

A mesmerising performance

Left: Elvis at a press conference in the International Hotel after the first night of his Las Vegas show. His performance had just finished with four standing ovations, and critics were soon speaking of "a mesmerising performance." He told journalists, "I'm really glad to be back in front of a live audience. I don't think I have ever been more excited than I was tonight."

Opposite: Elvis chats to his father, Vernon Presley, at the press conference. Elvis had been on a diet to lose weight and to get fit before the Las Vegas run, so he was looking handsome, healthy, and full of energy. At this stage he was at the peak of his singing career, and fans traveled from all over the world to see the Las Vegas shows.

"In the Ghetto" hits Gold

Opposite: Just before his appearance in Las Vegas, the RIAA had certified Elvis's latest single, "In The Ghetto," as a gold record. The song came about after big changes were made in how Elvis recorded. His sessions in the big Nashville studio had not been going well, and much of the material had to be discarded. Meanwhile a small, new studio had started up in Memphis; American had had a string of hits under the direction of Chips Moman. Elvis was persuaded to try them out, and he was soon recording some of his best material.

Above: A sleek and slim Elvis on stage in Las Vegas. By the end of the first Vegas run, fans were going wild every night and throwing their underwear onto the stage. The success of "In the Ghetto" was quickly followed by "Suspicious Minds," which became an Elvis classic. Both of these songs were selected by Chips Moman from his own library for Elvis to try, and he recorded them without the approval of the Colonel. The American sessions also led to "Don't Cry, Daddy," which went to Gold as well, but Elvis was never to be so adventurous again.

A marriage in difficulties

Opposite: Elvis at Graceland. Although his career was back on track, the same could not be said for Elvis's personal life. Priscilla was often absent from his side in public, but at first this was explained away by telling everyone that she was busy overseeing work on a new house that was being built in Monovale. Elvis did not lack for company—there were always women only too pleased to be with him. Often it was just company he was after; many of his so-called "girlfriends" said later that nothing happened, he just did not want to sleep alone.

Above: A happy family snapshot, but appearances were deceptive. In November 1970 Elvis told the press that his marriage was going through a difficult patch: it certainly had not helped when a Hollywood waitress, Patricia Parker, claimed that Elvis was the father of her son and filed a paternity suit. In the event, a blood test proved that Elvis was not the father, and the suit was dropped. Despite their problems, Elvis believed that Priscilla would stay around on his terms—it didn't occur to him that she might leave him for another man.

ELVIS PRESLEY

November 1970: Elvis, That's The Way It Is

Opposite and right: Two stills from *That's The Way It Is*, a documentary showing Elvis on tour. The filmmakers, Bob Abel and Pierre Adidge, had the most up to date mobile cameras and other state-of-the-art equipment and they followed Elvis around for some time, recording him as if he were a mythical hero on a quest. As well as recording performances, they showed life backstage, candid footage and highlights from the past. The resulting film was a refreshing record of Elvis at his peak, full of spontaneity and movement. The two filmmakers had even won over Colonel Parker, who said "Go out there and make the best film ever." And that is pretty much what they did—even today, the documentary is one of the classic records of a star on tour.

Thank you, Mr President

Opposite: Elvis meets with President Richard Nixon, in December 1970. Some time previously voice-over artist Paul Frees had revealed that he was an undercover narcotics agent and had an official Bureau of Narcotics and Dangerous Drugs badge to prove it. Elvis immediately wanted a BNDD badge of his own and tried to get one from the Bureau—and when he was turned down he simply asked the President for one instead. He not only received the coveted badge, but was invited the White House for a personal meeting.

Above: In August 1970 there had been a threat to kidnap or kill Elvis during a show, which turned out to be a hoax. However, Elvis became paranoid about security, and was sworn in as a special deputy so he could carry a gun. Typically he threw himself into a new interest with enthusiasm, and soon began collecting guns and police badges. Here he poses with the male members of Sonny West's wedding party, all proudly displaying their deputy's badges. Elvis had walked up the aisle as best man wearing a good selection of his collection of firearms.

June 1972: Opening at Madison Square Garden

Opposite: Elvis appeared at Madison Square Garden in New York for the first time in 1972. There were four concerts, which were followed by a short tour. He was noticeably much heavier and less fit than he had been for the *Comeback Special* four years earlier. Despite this, the Madison Square Garden concerts were a great success—all four performances were sold out, which meant a total of 80,000 people came to see him sing. After so many years of making movies Elvis was delighted to get back to performing on stage. At a press conference in 1973 he was to say, "A live concert to me is exciting because of all the electricity that is generated in the crowd and on stage. It's my favorite part of the business —live concerts."

Right: Another reporter at the press conference asked Elvis if he was happy with his image. Elvis told him that there was a difference between the image and the human being—and that it was very difficult to live up to an image. This was obviously something he had thought about and would continue to think about—a few years later producer Felton Jarvis was surprised when Elvis turned to him out of the blue and said, "I'm just so tired of being Elvis Presley." He was not the only one tired of Elvis Presley—Priscilla had left him in December 1971, although it wasn't until the following February that she told him that she was having a affair with karate instructor Mike Stone.

January 1973: Aloha From Hawaii

Above: After all the recent successes, the Colonel soon came up with an even bigger project, which was not only massive in scale but also innovative in concept. Elvis had been wanting to do a worldwide tour for some time, but for whatever reason this had never come off. Instead the Colonel arranged the next best thing—a television special in Hawaii that would be beamed live by satellite to countries all over the world. It was also recorded, so it could be re-transmitted a few days later to all those countries that had missed the live version.

Opposite: The programme was not shown in America until April 4, 1973, on NBC, when it attracted 51 percent of the television viewing audience. It was seen in more American households than man's first walk on the moon, and in around 40 countries by nearly 1.5 billion people. Elvis was enthusiastic about the project from the beginning, and he lost weight beforehand so he looked slim, fit and handsome. He also picked out some new songs to sing, and the soundtrack album quickly went to No. 1 on the *Billboard* album chart.

Aloha Linda

Opposite: Elvis and Priscilla were legally separated in July 1972, and in August Elvis filed for divorce. In July he had met Linda Thompson, who was the reigning Miss Tennessee, and whose sunny personality seemed to calm his bad moods. By September, Linda had moved into Graceland and she was to remain with Elvis for the next three years. For the last couple of years Elvis had been behaving erratically, both in public and private—mainly due to the number and mixture of prescription drugs he was taking—but now everyone hoped that he had turned a corner toward better things.

Right: The promising signs that Elvis had sorted himself out were an illusion, unfortunately. In February 1973 he missed several concerts during his season at Las Vegas, as the mix of prescription drugs began to affect his health. Later in the year several scheduled concerts in a season of 25 at the Sahara Tahoe Hotel in Stateline, Nevada, were also canceled. Elvis was treated by several doctors, and the Colonel even hired a private investigator to try to find out where he was getting his supply of drugs.

ELVIS
RIAA

The Madison Square Garden album goes Platinum

Opposite: Elvis receiving his Platinum record. He was now performing a grueling schedule of concerts with little rest in between, despite his poor health. Things were bound to go wrong, and soon they did. On stage in Las Vegas, Elvis made several critical comments about the management of the Hilton—who were now the owners of the International—and the Colonel was furious. After the show the two of them had a major row and the Colonel quit at the same moment as Elvis fired him. They did not speak to each other for several weeks, although they did eventually make up.

Right: Priscilla and Elvis leave the court in Santa Monica after their divorce is finalized on October 9, 1973. Priscilla said later that even after the divorce they remained close and that Elvis was always an exceptionally caring father. A few days later Elvis suffered a serious reaction to the drugs he was taking and collapsed—although the newspapers put it down to the emotional trauma of the divorce.

The jumpsuits

Opposite: Elvis in one of his signature jumpsuits, which came to symbolized the 1970s era of his career. Many of the jumpsuits were designed by Bill Belew, who had first met Elvis when designing the costumes for the *'68 Comeback Special*. Elvis wanted an outfit to wear on stage that would be easy to wear and comfortable, but which would allow him plenty of freedom of movement. The suits were decorated with studs, semi-precious stones and embroidery and they became increasingly elaborate. Many of the suits were given names: this one is known as the Red Lion or sometimes as the White Pinwheel.

Right: The themes used for the costumes were often of special significance to Elvis, and included karate symbols, tigers, peacocks and the phoenix. The costume for *Aloha from Hawaii* had an American eagle, as a patriotic message to the rest of the world. The costume shown right is known as the White Prehistoric Bird Suit or the White Bicentennial Suit, but is being worn with the Indian Head Belt. There was also a blue version of this jumpsuit design, which had white sleeves.

1973: On tour

Opposite and right: Throughout 1973, Elvis performed a punishing tour and recording schedule with very little rest. In March 1973 the Colonel sold the singer's royalty rights on Elvis' entire recording catalog up to that point to RCA for 5.4 million dollars. Many asked why Elvis did not slow down, but the truth was that he had a very expensive lifestyle to support. As well as his family members he had a large entourage, all relying on him to support them. He was also extremely generous to strangers—he often gave away brand new cars, expensive jewelry and money, often on a whim. As fast as the money was earned it was spent, so there was always a need to earn more money. Elvis had become bored with life on the road and wanted a new challenge, but nothing that came along seemed quite right. His general health was also not very good—as he had glaucoma in one eye, recurring pneumonia and pleurisy, an enlarged colon, and hepatitis. At the end of October he spent two weeks in hospital in Memphis, where he was also put through a drug withdrawal program.

Turning over a new leaf

Left: At the beginning of 1974 Elvis was slimmer and fitter than he had been for some time. When he began touring Dr. Nichopoulos came with him to keep an eye on his drug intake. The doctor worked out a daily regime that would give Elvis what he needed, but which replaced some drugs with placebos if he thought Elvis didn't really need them. Part of the problem was that because the drugs were all originally prescribed for a genuine reason, Elvis would never accept that he now had an addiction problem.

Opposite: A smiling Elvis looks on top of the world. In March 1974 he returned to play the Houston Astrodome, and the two shows broke the previous one-day attendance record. He also performed in Memphis for the first time since 1961, doing four shows in two days because of the outstanding demand for tickets. One of the shows was recorded for a new album: *Elvis Recorded Live On Stage in Memphis*. It included the live performance of "How Great Thou Art" that brought Elvis his third Grammy award. Although things looked as if they were going well, it was not long before Elvis started gaining weight again.

1975: Looking exhausted

Opposite: Elvis at a concert in Asheville in July 1975. He had turned 40 in January 1975, and was depressed and overweight. At the end of the month he had been rushed to hospital with severe stomach pains and was admitted to get his drug intake under control. A week later Vernon had a heart attack and joined him in the same hospital. After they were both discharged, Elvis went back to Graceland to try and rest and lose more weight, but his good resolutions did not last. Efforts were being made to stop him getting drugs, but they were not successful.

Right: Putting on weight was an expression of boredom for Elvis, but since he was also older he naturally found it less easy to shed any excess pounds. His general health problems had slowed him down, so he was not burning up calories like he used to, but he still lived on a diet of junk food. At concerts he sometimes appeared exhausted, but despite his bloated appearance he was still Elvis, and the die-hard fans loved him.

1976: Goodbye Linda, hello Ginger

Opposite: Elvis with Linda Thompson, in March 1976. Linda had been his steady girlfriend since 1972, but by now she had realized that she could not save Elvis from himself. In November the two of them split up for good, but he soon met someone new: Ginger Alden, who was also a former beauty queen. Ginger was his steady girlfriend until his death. The touring schedule was still as packed as ever but Elvis often seemed uninterested on stage and would stop singing and simply talk to the audience.

Above: Elvis leads a convoy of Memphis Mafia members, all driving three-wheelers, out of the gates of Graceland. The Mafia was now depleted, as Vernon had fired Red and Sonny West and Dave Hebler, citing a lack of funds and a need to cut expenses. The three of them did not go quietly—they soon teamed up with journalist Steve Dunleavy to write a sensational book that detailed what life had been like around Elvis. Elvis not only felt betrayed; he was also concerned about what outsiders would make of some of the weirder revelations.

August 1977: Elvis has left the building

Opposite: On June 26, 1977, Elvis appeared in a concert at Indiana's Market Square Arena in Indianapolis—it would be his very last concert performance. He returned to Graceland to rest, and to spend some time with Lisa Marie, who was there on a two-week visit. Very late on August 15 he visited his dentist, returning after midnight and finally settling down to try and sleep in the early hours of the 16th. He was due to fly to Portland, Maine that evening to start a scheduled tour, but later in the morning Ginger came to look for him and found him dead.

Above: Elvis's funeral was a private service at Graceland, but thousands gathered outside to pay their respects. A white hearse carried his body to Forest Hill Cemetery, followed by a cortege of 49 cars. He was buried next to his mother, but after three men attempted to dig up the coffin—apparently to try and prove that Elvis was not really dead—both Elvis and his mother were moved to the Meditation Garden at Graceland. The garden also includes a memorial plaque for Elvis's stillborn twin brother, and Vernon was buried there after his death in 1979.

The King is dead, long live the King

Above : Fans gather at Graceland in 2007 on the 30th anniversary of Elvis's death. The entire estate was left to his daughter Lisa Marie in trust until she was 25, but there was no money left. In an effort to raise some, Graceland was opened to the public in 1982 and is now one of the most visited historic homes in America, second only to the White House. The Presley estate began to collect any income that was being generated through using Elvis's name, and over the following years it has earned far more money than Elvis ever did in his lifetime.

Opposite: Elvis's living room at Graceland, with the specially-designed stained glass peacock panels. The trophy room—which today is a tribute to Elvis's incredible success, displaying his Gold and Platinum disks, other awards and a selection of his clothing—was originally used by Elvis to race slot cars. Tours of the mansion cover many rooms on the ground floor, including the music room, dining room, TV room, kitchen and jungle room, but upstairs is not open to the public—even when Elvis was alive, it was regarded as his inner sanctum.

Living a dream

Opposite: Elvis as the fans like to remember him. He is perhaps even more famous today than he was when he was alive: the shops are full of his records, there has been a constant stream of documentaries and films about him, and his better movies and the major TV specials are often still broadcast on television. Several of his records have been re-released and have entered the charts, while the classics have continued to sell well, earning more Gold and Platinum disks.

Above: Elvis Presley's star on the Walk of Fame in Hollywood. He has also been posthumously inducted into the Rock 'n' Roll, Country and Gospel Halls of Fame—the first singer to achieve all three. But today he is far more than just a singer, or an actor, or a worldwide star with an amazing lifestyle—he is an American folk hero. As Elvis once said, "When I was a child I was a dreamer. I read comic books, and I was the hero of the comic book. I saw movies, and I was the hero in the movie. So every dream I have ever dreamed has come true a thousand times."

Chronology and Filmography

CHRONOLOGY

1933

Jun 17 The wedding day of Vernon Elvis Presley and Gladys Love Smith

1935

Jan 8 Elvis Aaron Presley is born at 306 Old Saltillo Road, the home of his parents. His twin brother is stillborn

1938

May 25 After being found guilty of forging a check, Vernon Presley is sentenced to serve 3 years at Parchman penal plantation, a Mississippi state penitentiary. Vernon is released early for good behavior in October 1940

1945

Jan 8 Elvis is given a guitar for his tenth birthday

Oct 3 Elvis sings "Old Shep" in a competition at the annual Mississippi–Alabama Fair and Dairy Show, held in Tupelo, Mississippi. He wins second-place prize of $5 along with free admission to the fair's rides

1949

Sept 20 The Presleys move to Memphis and manage a settled life for nearly three years

1951

Jun 3 Elvis starts work at Precision Tools, but is fired the following month when it is learned he too young to be employed

1953

May 26 Elvis performs at the *First Jimmie Rodgers Memorial Talent Show* in Meridian, Mississippi, winning second-place guitar with a country version of "I'm Left, You're Right, She's Gone" and a rock-style "Baby, Let's Play House"

Summer At Sam Phillips's Memphis Recording Service Elvis records "My Happiness" and "That's When Your Heartache Begins." He takes the original with him; no copies are made

1954

Jan 4 Elvis records "I'll Never Stand in Your Way" and "Casual Love Affair" but again he takes the original and there are no copies made

Jan Elvis starts to date Dixie Locke, his first serious girlfriend

May Sam Phillips asks Elvis to sing "Without You," then calls guitarist Scotty Moore and bass player Bill Black and puts them to work with Elvis. The three rehearse at Sun Studios for several weeks

Jul 5—6 At Sun Studios Elvis, Scotty Moore and Bill Black record "That's All Right, Mama" and "Blue Moon of Kentucky"

Jul 7 Sam Phillips circulates demos of the record, and DJ Dewey Phillips plays "That's All Right, Mama" on WHBQ 14 times in succession. and interviews Elvis on air

Jul 12 Elvis's parents sign a one-year contract on his behalf, with Scotty Moore

Jul 19 Official release of "That's All Right, Mama"/"Blue Moon of Kentucky," which has soon sold 20,000 copies

Jul 30 Elvis appears at the Overton Park Shell, his first major concert

Aug 7 *Billboard* gives "That's All Right, Mama," a good review

Sep 25 Elvis and the Blue Moon Boys appear at the *Grand Ole Opry*, but are not well received so Elvis never performs there again

Oct Elvis is brought to the attention of Colonel Tom Parker by promoter Oscar "The Baron" Davis. The Colonel comes to see him perform, after which they meet at Taylor's restaurant with Scotty, Bill Black, the Baron and Bob Neal

Oct 16 Elvis and the Blue Moon Boys appear on the *Louisiana Hayride*, a radio show broadcast across the southern U.S. by KWKH from the Municipal Auditorium at Shreveport. They are an immediate success and are soon performing weekly

Nov The band goes on a concert tour through Texas, appearing at Boston, Lufkin, Longview, Odessa and the Memphis Airport Inn

Dec 18 "I'm Left, You're Right, She's Gone" and "My Baby's Gone" are both recorded at Sun Studios

1955

Jan 8 Release of "Milkcow Blues Boogie"/"You're a Heartbreaker," which does not go into the charts

Jan Colonel Parker sends Jimmy Rodgers Snow, Hank Williams' son, to see Elvis perform. He reports back that Elvis is provocative, sexy and appeals to all women

Mar The band flies to New York City to audition for Arthur Godfrey's *Talent Scouts*, but are turned down

Mar 5 Elvis makes his TV debut when the *Louisiana Hayride* is broadcast from Shreveport, Louisiana

Mar 14 Country singing star Jimmy Dean interviews Elvis for *Town and Country Jubilee*, a radio show on WMAL

Mar 19 Elvis appears live on KPRC-TV's *Grand Prize Saturday Night Jamboree*, broadcast from Eagle's Hall in Houston, Texas—where he also records "I Got a Woman"

Apr 1 "Baby, Let's Play House"/"I'm Left, You're Right, She's Gone" is released and the A side causes a stir as it appears to hint at premarital sex

Jun 26 Elvis meets June Juanico after a concert in Biloxi, Mississippi, and dates her on and off for a year

Jul "Baby, Let's Play House" makes it into *Billboard*'s Top Ten

Aug 6 Release of "I forgot to Remember to Forget"/"Mystery Train," which goes into *Billboard*'s country chart for 40 weeks

Aug 15 Although he is still bound to Bob Neal for another year, Elvis signs a contract giving Colonel Parker the right to manage his career

Sept "Mystery Train" enters *Billboard*'s country chart, where it stays for 30 weeks

Nov 10 At the annual DJ convention in Nashville, Elvis secures the recording rights to "Heartbreak Hotel" from Mae Axton

Nov 13 The Country & Western Disc Jockey Association names Elvis "Most Promising Country Artist"

Nov 20 Elvis's contract with Sun Records is bought for $35,000 by RCA Victor. Sam Phillip's Hi-Lo Music publishing company is bought by Hill & Range Music for $15,000

Nov 22 Elvis signs a contract that makes Colonel Parker his exclusive representative

1956

Jan 5 Colonel Parker establishes a 50/50 partnership for five years to publish the songs Elvis records, between with Hill & Range Music and the newly created Presley Music Inc.

Jan 10 After rehearsing "Heartbreak Hotel" the previous day, Elvis records it for RCA along with "I got a Woman." The next day he records "I Was the One" and "I'm Counting on You"

Jan 17 Release of "Heartbreak Hotel"/"I Was the One"

Jan 28 Elvis appears on Milton Berle's *Stage Show* on CBS TV

Jan 30—31 During a 2-day studio session "Blue Suede Shoes" is recorded

Feb 4 Elvis appears on the Dorsey Brothers' *Stage Show* on CBS TV

Feb 15 Both "I forgot to Remember to Forget"/"Mystery Train" reach No 1 on *Billboard*'s country chart, the first Elvis records to do so

Feb 22 "Heartbreak Hotel" enters *Billboard*'s Top 100 chart at No 68 and the Country's Best Sellers in Stores chart at No 9

Feb 29 "I Was the One" enters *Billboard*'s Top 100 chart at No 84

Mar 1 362,000 advance orders are received for the first LP, *Elvis Presley*, and RCA is overwhelmed

Mar 7 "Heartbreak Hotel" is No 1 on *Billboard*'s Country Best Sellers in Stores chart

Mar 13 The LP, *Elvis Presley*, is released and stays in *Billboard*'s Extended-play album chart for a total of 68 weeks. It goes on to become the first in history to sell a million copies

Mar 15 Colonel Parker officially becomes sole manager of Elvis

Mar 28 "Blue Suede Shoes" enters *Billboard*'s Top 100 chart at No 88

Apr 1 Elvis does a screen test in Los Angeles, for Hal Wallis at Paramount Pictures

Apr 3 Elvis appears on *The Milton Berle Show*, singing on the deck of USS *Hancock* in San Diego, California

Apr "Heartbreak Hotel" is No 1 on *Billboard*'s Pop chart and stays there for seven weeks. At the same time it is No 1 on the Country & Western chart and No 5 on the R&B chart

Apr 6 Paramount Pictures contracts Elvis for 7 years, to make 3 movies

Apr 11 *Variety* claims that "Heartbreak Hotel" is the first Elvis record to sell one million copies

May "I Want You, I Need You, I Love You"/"My Baby Left Me" is released and stays in *Billboard*'s Top 100 chart for 24 weeks, reaching No 3. It also gets to No 10 on the R&B chart and for one week is No 1 on the Country chart.

Jun 5 A second appearance on *The Milton Berle Show*

Jul 1 Elvis sings "Hound Dog" to a basset hound on *The Steve Allen Show*

Aug 20 Elvis begins work on his first movie, *Love Me Tender*, for Twentieth-Century Fox

Sep 5 "Don't Be Cruel"/"Hound Dog" hits No 1 on *Billboard*'s Top 100 chart

Sep 9 When Elvis appears on *The Ed Sullivan Show* it gets the highest ratings in television history

Sep 19 "Blue Moon" enters *Billboard*'s Top 100 chart at No 87

Sep 26 Tupelo's Elvis Presley Day

Oct *Variety* names Elvis "King of Rock 'n' Roll" and he also appears on the cover of *Rock and Roll* magazine

Oct Elvis receives a draft questionnaire

Oct 3 "I Don't Care If the Sun Don't Shine" enters *Billboard*'s Top 100 chart at No 77

Oct 8 It is revealed in *Time* magazine that RCA has advance orders of one million for the single of "Love Me Tender"—a record high

Oct 10 "Love Me Tender"/ "Any Way You Want Me" enters *Billboard*'s Top 100 chart at No 9

Oct 19 Release of the LP *Elvis*

Oct 24 Elvis earns his 5th gold record of that year for "Love Me Tender"

Nov The EPs *Elvis Vol 1* and *Elvis Vol 2* are released

Nov 7 The LP *Elvis* enters *Billboard*'s Best Selling Packaged Records–Popular Albums at No 7 and "Love Me Tender" reaches No 1 on the Top 100 chart

Nov 15 The movie *Love Me Tender* opens in 500 theatres across the U.S. and is a smash hit

Nov 21 Colonel Parker owns Elvis completely, after he gets Bob Neal to sign a contract to that effect, and pays off Hank Snow in lieu of a finder's fee

Nov 28 The movie *Love Me Tender* enters *Variety*'s National Box Office Survey at No 2

Dec Release of the EP *Love Me Tender*

Dec 15 Elvis appears for the last time at the *Louisiana Hayride*

Dec *Billboard*'s No 1 single for 1956 is "Heartbreak Hotel"

1957

Jan 4 Elvis has his preinduction Army physical at Kennedy Veterans Hospital, and is classed 1-A for draft

Jan 6 A final appearance on *The Ed Sullivan Show*

Jan 21 *Loving You* begins shooting for Paramount

Jan "Too Much"/"Playing for Keeps" is released, staying at No 2 for four weeks in *Billboard*'s Top 100 chart, and remaining in the chart for 17 weeks

Mar 7 Elvis buys Graceland, outbidding the YMCA by offering $102,500

Apr 10 "All Shook Up" hits the No 1 spot on *Billboard*'s Top 100 chart—and holds it for eight weeks

May 13 *Jailhouse Rock* begins filming for MGM, in Culver City

June Release of the first Elvis single to be distributed in the UK, "Teddy Bear"/"Loving You," which goes on to sell over one million copies

Sep "Jailhouse Rock"/"Treat Me Nice" is released in the UK and becomes the first Elvis record to enter the charts at No I in England. It is already released in the U.S. and it goes on to sell over three million copies in 12 months

Jul 9 *Loving You* has its première at the Strand Theatre in Memphis.

Jul 27 After reaching the No 1 spot on *Billboard*'s Top 100 chart, "Teddy Bear"/"Loving You" stays there for 17 weeks. It also makes No 1 for one week on both the R&B and Country charts

Aug 30 *The Spokane Review* reports that 12,000 fans were whipped to frenzy at a concert in the local Memorial Stadium. Fans try to steal soil from the infield, where Elvis's feet had rested

Sep Scotty Moore and Bill Black leave Elvis because of the poor pay and lack of credit, although they play at some further recording sessions

Sep 27 At Tupelo's Mississippi–Alabama Fair and Dairy Show, Elvis plays at a concert to benefit the Elvis

Presley Youth Recreation Center, which he goes on to establish in his home town that December

Sep 28 The LP *Elvis Presley* reaches No 1 on *Billboard*'s Extended-play-album chart and stays there for six weeks

Oct 17 *Jailhouse Rock* has its première in Memphis, and opens across the country on November 8. It goes on to make a profit within three weeks

Dec 19 Elvis receives his draft notice

1958

Mar 5 *King Creole* starts filming for Paramount

Mar 24 After being inducted into the Army, Elvis is sent to Fort Chaffee, Arkansas. An Army haircut removes the famous duck-tail and sideburns

Mar 28 Along with other recruits, Elvis is sent to Fort Hood for basic training

Jul 1 Release of *King Creole*

Aug 5 Elvis's mother, Gladys is rushed to hospital and he is granted compassionate leave

Aug 11 "Hard Headed Woman" is the first Elvis song to receive a RIAA Gold Disk Award

Aug 14 Gladys dies in hospital. Her funeral is held in Memphis two days later and she is buried at Forest Hill Cemetery

Aug 24 Elvis returns to basic training, since his unit is soon being sent to Germany,

Sep 19 Elvis travels from Fort Hood to Brooklyn, New York, with his Army unit

Sept 22 The unit leave on the USS *General Randall* for Bremerhaven, Germany. Here they disembark to transfer to the base at Friedberg

Oct 2 Elvis gives a Press conference at the Thirty-second Armored Battalion in Friedberg, Germany. Vernon and Minnie Mae Presley have come with Elvis and stay near where he is stationed, along with Red West and Lamar Fike

Nov 27 Elvis receives his first promotion, to private first class

Dec Elvis is awarded "World's Outstanding Popular Singer," "World's Outstanding Musical Personality" and "Favorite US Male Singer," for 1958

1959

Jan 8 On his 24th birthday, Elvis is called by Dick Clark, who tells him he has been voted "Best Singer of the Year," and that "King Creole" is "Best Song of the Year." That evening Dick Clark's *American Bandstand* program is dedicated to Elvis

Jun 1 Elvis receives a second promotion, to specialist fourth class

Nov Elvis and Priscilla Beaulieu are introduced at a party

1960

Jan 20 Elvis receives a fourth promotion, to sergeant, and gets a raise of $22.94 a month

Feb The magazine *Elvis Monthly* is released in the United States

Feb 17 The LP *Elvis* is certified by the RIAA as a Gold Disk—although it has already sold more than three million copies

Mar 2 Elvis flies out of Germany from Wiesbaden airport, arriving at McGuire Air Force Base at Fort Dix the next day

Mar 3 A photo of Elvis in uniform is featured on the front pages of newspapers across America.

Mar 26 Elvis tapes "The Frank Sinatra–Timex Special" in the Grand Ballroom of the Fontainbleau Hotel, Miami Beach. It also includes a host of other stars including Nancy Sinatra, Sammy Davis Jr. and Peter Lawford and is broadcast on May 12 on ABC TV

Apr 3 The LP *Elvis is Back* is released and reaches No 2 in *Billboard*'s Best-Selling chart. It stays in the chart for a total of 56 weeks

Apr 3 "It's Now or Never"/"A Mess of Blues" is recorded. It enters *Billboard*'s Hot 100 chart at No 44 but climbs to No 1 within five weeks. It remains in the chart for 20 weeks, and also reaches No 7 on the R&B chart. It is *Billboard*'s Vocal Single of 1960 and carries on selling through the years, reaching well over 23 million copies

Apr 4 "Are You Lonesome Tonight" is recorded. It breaks records by entering *Billboard*'s Hot 100 chart at No 35 but jumping to No 2 within seven days. It stays in the chart for 16 weeks, and also reaches No 22 on the Country chart, No 3 on the R&B chart and staying at No 1 in the English charts for four weeks

May 2 *G.I. Blues* begins shooting for Paramount

Jul 3 Elvis's father, Vernon, marries Dee Stanley, an American woman he met in Germany. Elvis does not attend the wedding

Aug 15 Filming begins on *Flaming Star* for Twentieth Century Fox

Oct 30 "It's Now or Never"/"A Mess of Blues" goes in at No 1 in the English charts, and stays there for eight weeks

Nov 11 *Wild in the Country* begins shooting for Twentieth Century Fox

Nov 23 Release of *G.I. Blues* nationwide. It reaches No 2 in *Variety*'s list of top-grossing films

Nov 23 A version of *Flaming Star* with only two songs is previewed and is later selected for general release. It hits No 12 in Variety's list of top-grossing films

1961

Mar 17 *Blue Hawaii* begins shooting for Paramount

Mar 25 A benefit concert for the USS *Arizona* Memorial Fund, held at Bloch Arena in Pearl Harbor, Hawaii, raises $65,000

Jun 15 *Wild in the Country* has its première and is released nationwide on June 22.

Jul 11 *Follow That Dream* begins shooting for United Artists

Nov 5—14 Former junior-welterweight champion Mush Callahan coaches Elvis for the boxing scenes in *Kid Galahad*

Nov *Kid Galahad* begins shooting for United Artists

Nov 21 Nationwide release of *Blue Hawaii*. Within a month it has grossed $4.7 million

1962

Apr 9 *Girls! Girls! Girls!* begins shooting for Paramount

Apr 11 *Follow That Dream* is premièred in Ocala, Florida. It is released nationwide on May 23

June Priscilla Beaulieu arrives in Los Angeles from Germany

Aug 27 *It Happened at the World's Fair* begins shooting for MGM

Aug 29 *Kid Galahad* is released nationwide and has grossed $1.7 million by the end of the year

Sep 8 Elvis comes to Seattle for location filming on *It Happened at the World's Fair*

Oct "Return to Sender"/"Where Do You Come From?" is released. It hits No 2 on *Billboard*'s Hot 100 chart, No 5 on the R&B chart and sits at No 1 for three weeks in the UK

Oct 31 *Girls! Girls! Girls!* premières in Honolulu and is released nationwide on Nov 21. It goes on to gross $2.6 million by the end of the year

Dec Elvis receives three Norwegian Silver Record Awards for "Good Luck Charm" and is voted fifth top box-office draw by theater owners

Dec Priscilla visits America and spends Christmas with Elvis at Graceland

1963

Jan Priscilla goes back to Germany, but Elvis begins pressing her family to allow her to move to America and finish her education in Memphis

Jan 28 *Fun in Acapulco* begins shooting for Paramount.

Mar Priscilla begins schooling at the Immaculate Conception High School, a Catholic all-girl establishment

Apr 3 *It Happened at the World's Fair* premières in Los Angeles, and opens nationwide on April 10. It grosses $2.25 million by the end of the year

Jul 15 *Viva Las Vegas* begins shooting for MGM; during the filming Elvis and his co-star Ann-Margret become close

Oct 5 *Kissin' Cousins* begins shooting for MGM

Nov 27 *Fun in Acapulco* is released nationwide; it gross over $1.5 million within a month

Dec 11 The movie *Love Me Tender* is shown on television

1964

Feb 7 Elvis sends The Beatles a message of congratulations when they arrive in New York

Feb 15 Elvis donates the yacht Potomac to St Jude's Children's Hospital

Mar 9 *Roustabout* begins shooting for Paramount

Apr National release of *Kissin' Cousins*

Apr *The Elvis Echo* newspaper, edited by Paulette Sansone, is first published

Apr 20 *Viva Las Vegas* premières in New York and is released nationwide on June 17. It grosses over $4.5 million by the end of the year; *Roustabout* finishes shooting

Jun 22 *Girl Happy* begins shooting for MGM. The following month Elvis receives a South African Gold Record Award for "Kiss Me Quick" on the MGM lot

Oct 6 *Tickle Me* begins shooting for Allied Artists

Nov 11 *Roustabout* is released nationwide. It goes on to gross $3 million by the end of December

Dec Elvis is voted sixth top box-office draw by theater owners

Dec Tennessee state senator LeRoy Johnson presents Elvis with an award as the state's "Entertainer of the Year"

1965

Jan 8 Elvis's 30th birthday, which he celebrates at Graceland

Mar 15 *Harum Scarum* begins shooting for MGM

Apr 14 *Girl Happy* goes on general release; it grosses $3.1 million by the end of the year, despite poor reviews

May 25 *Frankie and Johnny* begins shooting for United Artists

May 28 *Tickle Me* premières in Atlanta, Georgia

Aug 7 *Paradise, Hawaiian Style* begins shooting

Aug 15 Colonel Parker and Elvis lay two wreaths at the USS *Arizona* memorial

Nov 24 *Harum Scarum* premières in Los Angeles

Dec Elvis moves to Rocca Place in Stone Canyon from Perugia Way, Bel Air

Dec Elvis is voted sixth top box-office draw by theater owners, and pop polls name him as top musical personality

1966

Feb 20 *Spinout* begins shooting for MGM, and finishes on April 6

Mar 31 *Frankie and Johnny* premières in Baton Rouge, Louisiana

May A short promotional film for *Paradise, Hawaiian Style* is released

Jun *Paradise Hawaiian Style* is selected as "Picture of the Month" by *Seventeen* magazine. It goes on nationwide release on July 6 and grosses over $2.5 million by the end of the year

Jun 11 *Double Trouble* begins shooting for MGM and finishes on September 5

Sep 12 *Easy Come, Easy Go* begins shooting for Paramount. Filming finishes on October 28

Nov 1 The LP *Elvis Presley* is certified as a Platinum Disk by the RIAA after it has sold a million copies

Nov 23 *Spinout* is released nationwide

Dec Elvis is voted tenth top box-office draw by theater owners—it is the last time he appears in the poll.

Dec Elvis finally proposes to Priscilla

1967

Feb 9 Elvis purchases a ranch in Walls, Mississippi

Mar *Clambake* begins shooting for United Artists, in Los Angeles

Mar 22 *Easy Come, Easy Go* opens nationwide and has grossed over $1.95 million by the end of the year

Apr 5 *Double Trouble* goes nationwide and soon grosses $1.6 million

May 1 Elvis and Priscilla Beaulieu are married in a private ceremony at the Aladdin Hotel in Las Vegas

May 7 After their honeymoon, Elvis and Priscilla move into Hillcrest Road, Beverly Hills

May 29 Graceland hosts a second wedding ceremony for the people excluded from the Las Vegas one

Aug Elvis and Priscilla feature on the front covers of *Movie Life, Cineavance* and *Movieland*

Oct 18 *Stay Away, Joe* begins shooting for MGM in Arizona

Nov 22 *Clambake* is released nationwide but gets poor reviews

Dec 8 *Tickle Me* is featured in CBS-TV's *Friday Night at the Movies*

Dec Elvis receives a Grammy Award for Best Sacred Performance for "How Great Thou Art" and a pop poll names him the No 1 Male Singer and No 1 Music Personality in America

1968

Feb 1 Elvis and Priscilla have a daughter, Lisa Marie Presley, at the Baptist Memorial Hospital

Feb 8 In their feature on the year's music scene, *Playboy* magazine honors Elvis

Mar 8 *Stay Away, Joe* is released nationwide

May 25 Elvis meets martial arts expert Mike Stone and suggests he teaches Priscilla karate

May Priscilla gives Elvis a 1928 Kimball grand piano with gold-leaf inside and out on their first wedding anniversary

Jun 12 *Speedway* begins shooting for MGM. It also stars Nancy Sinatra

Jun 15 Elvis and Priscilla fly to Honolulu to see the USS *Arizona* Memorial

Jun 27—30 Elvis is filmed for a Christmas TV special to be broadcast on NBC-TV, in which he goes back to his musical roots

Jul *Live a Little, Love a Little* begins shooting for MGM, in Los Angeles

Jul 22 *Charro!* begins shooting for National General, in Arizona

Oct 23 *Live a Little, Love a Little* is released nationwide

Oct 28 *The Trouble with Girls* begins shooting for MGM

Dec 3 The *Comeback TV Special* is broadcast on NBC-TV and tops the ratings that week

Dec 31 The *Comeback TV Special* is shown in the UK on BBC 2

1969

Mar 10 *Change of Habit* begins shooting for Universal and NBC, in Los Angeles

Mar 13 Charro! is released nationwide

May 2 *Change of Habit* finishes shooting. It is the last Elvis feature film, as Elvis has decided that he wants to return to singing

May 21 Elvis sells the Flying Circle G Ranch; all the horses are moved to Graceland

Jun 15 The RIAA certify "In the Ghetto" as gold

Jul 31 Elvis appears live in concert, for the first time in eight years, at the International Hotel in Las Vegas. Some critics are not impressed with the Vegas shows—but the fans travel from all over the world to see him

Aug A Press conference is held after the Vegas opening night and in the following weeks *Rolling Stone* magazine tells readers that Elvis is "supernatural," while *Variety* dubs him a "superstar." *Newsweek* compliments him on his staying power

Sep Release of "Suspicious Minds"/"You'll Think of Me," which reaches No 1 in *Billboard*'s Top 100 chart in November for one week, and stays in the chart for 15 weeks

Sep 3 *The Trouble With Girls* is released nationwide

Nov 10 *Change of Habit* is released nationwide

Dec 12 The RIAA certify the LP *From Memphis to Vegas/From Vegas to Memphis* as Gold

1970

Jan 21 The RIAA certify "Don't Cry Daddy" as Gold after it has sold a million copies

Jan 26 Elvis opens at the International Hotel in Las Vegas, the first in a new season of 57 concerts

Feb 27 Elvis plays the first concert of a three-day booking at Houston Astrodome, to coincide with the Houston Livestock Show. He performs two shows a night throughout the booking.

Jun 1 Felton Jarvis resigns from RCA, moving over to manage Elvis's recording career

Aug 14 Patricia Parker, a Hollywood waitress, files a paternity suit against Elvis. Her son Jason is born on Oct 19

Aug 26 After threats to kidnap or kill Elvis during a show are received the FBI are called, but it turns out to be a hoax

Oct Elvis becomes a special deputy in Memphis so he can legally carry a gun. He also has 14-carat gold necklaces made for the members of the Memphis Mafia, with TCB—for Taking Care of Business—and a lightning-bolt insignia

Nov Elvis tells the Press that he and Priscilla are having marriage difficulties

Nov 11 *Elvis, That's The Way It Is*—a film of concerts and recording sessions — premières in Phoenix, Arizona

Dec 3 Elvis spends $20,000 on guns in a three day shopping spree

Dec 21 Elvis meets President Nixon at the White House and is given a Narcotics Bureau badge after he offers to work undercover to help stamp out both drug abuse and subversive elements in America

Dec 30 Elvis is given a permit to carry a gun in any state, after being taken on a tour of the FBI headquarters in Washington DC

1971

Jan 9 The Jaycees—members of the Junior Chamber of Commerce, a civic organization for business and community leaders—vote Elvis one of the Ten Outstanding Young Men of America. It is the only award that Elvis collects in person

Jan—Feb Elvis plays another season of concerts at the International Hotel in Las Vegas

Jun 1 Elvis's birthplace in Tupelo is opened to the public

Sep 8 The National Academy of Recording Arts and Sciences give The Bing Crosby Award to Elvis

Oct 24 A twelve-hour radio show, The Elvis Presley Story, is produced by Jerry Hopkins and Ron Jacobs

Oct *The National Insider* reports that Elvis has a drug problem

Nov A lie-detector test and blood test prove Elvis is not the father of Patricia Parker's son, and she drops her paternity suit

Dec 30 Elvis reveals that Priscilla has left him

1972

Jan—Feb Elvis plays another season of concerts at the International Hotel in Las Vegas

Apr A documentary, *Elvis on Tour*, is filmed over a series of concerts at Buffalo in New York, Detroit, Dayton, Knoxville, Hampton Roads in Virginia, Richmond, Roanoke, Indianapolis, Charlotte, Greensboro, Macon, Jacksonville, Little Rock, San Antonio and Albuquerque.

Jun 6 Elvis plays the first of a 4-concert booking at Madison Square Garden

Jul 6 Linda Thompson, a former beauty queen, meets Elvis

Jul 26 Elvis and Priscilla are legally separated and the following month Elvis files for divorce

Aug—Sep Elvis appears in the series of Las Vegas concerts

Sep Linda Thompson is now Elvis's official girlfriend and she moves into Graceland

Oct 20 *Change of Habit* is featured on NBC's *Friday Night at the Movies*

Nov 1 *Elvis on Tour* is released and grosses nearly half a million dollars in just one week

Dec A "Best Inspirational Performance" Grammy is awarded for the LP *He Touched Me*. *Elvis on Tour* is voted "Best Documentary of 1972" by the Hollywood Foreign Press Association and is nominated for a Golden Globe

1973

Jan 14 *Elvis: Aloha From Hawaii* is broadcast to 40 countries around the world, and the following day to a further 28 countries

Feb The interaction between all the drugs he is taking causes health problems, and Elvis misses several concerts in Las Vegas and is treated by a succession of doctors

Feb 18 At the midnight show four men rush onto the stage, apparently to attack Elvis—but they turn out to be over-excited fans

Apr 4 *Elvis: Aloha From Hawaii* is expanded and broadcast across the U.S. on NBC-TV as a TV special

May 4 Elvis is booked for a season of 25 concerts at the Sahara Tahoe Hotel in Stateline, Nevada but several are cancelled due to illness

May 13 Elvis donates money to the Barton Memorial Hospital in memory of his mother, after a special Mother's Day concert

Aug 6 The first concert in a planned series of 59 at the Las Vegas Hilton; Elvis misses two due to illness

Aug Colonel Parker and Elvis have a major argument and dissolve their partnership, but it is later re-instated

Oct 9 Elvis and Priscilla's divorce is finalized in Santa Monica

Oct Elvis reacts badly to some drugs and is hospitalized for two weeks, during which he is put through a drug withdrawal program

Nov *Movie World* reports that Elvis has collapsed after the divorce

Dec 10–16 Using a mobile recording unit provided by RCA, Elvis records several songs in a session at Stax Studios in Memphis

1974

Jan Colonel Parker and Elvis form Boxcar Records—as well as Boxcar Enterprises, which will handle the merchandising of Elvis-related products not connected to movies or records

Mar Dr George Nichopoulos (Dr Nick) attends Elvis full time during a concert tour so that he can monitor the drug intake.

May After concerts in San Bernadino and Fresno, Elvis plays a 22-concert booking at the Sahara Tahoe Hotel in Stateline, Nevada

Jun Another 21-day tour begins

Aug 19 The first concert in a series of 29 at the Las Vegas Hilton—but Elvis is ill and has to cancel two performances

Aug Sheila Ryan replaces Linda Thompson as Elvis's official girlfriend

Nov Elvis wins a Grammy for "Best Inspirational Performance" for "How Great Thou Art," which is featured on the LP *Elvis Recorded Live*

1975

Jan 29 Elvis is admitted to get his drug use back under control, after being rushed to hospital at midnight with severe stomach pains

Feb 5 Elvis's father Vernon is admitted to the same hospital after a heart attack

Mar 28 Elvis is considered for the costarring role in the remake of *A Star is Born* opposite Barbra Streisand, but the Colonel handles negotiations and the project founders

Apr Elvis buys a 96-passenger Convair 880 plane, which is named the Lisa Marie

May 5 Elvis raises $108,000 for hurricane survivors in McComb, Mississippi by playing a benefit concert at the State Fair Coliseum in Jackson, Mississippi

Aug Priscilla and Mike Stone split up and Priscilla begins her acting career. Elvis is still in poor health and is putting on weight

Aug 18 Most of a series of concerts at the Las Vegas Hilton are cancelled due to Elvis's poor health

Aug 21 Doctors attempt to resolve some of Elvis's medical problems and he is admitted to hospital for two weeks

Aug After Linda Thompson leaves to pursue her acting career, Elvis briefly dates Jo Cathy Brownlee

Nov 28 Linda Thompson returns briefly to support Elvis when he flies to Las Vegas to rehearse

Dec 30 *Faces* publishes an article about "the King" returning and features Elvis on the cover

Dec 31 A concert held on New Year's Eve concert in Pontiac, Michigan breaks previous receipt records

1976

Jan 22 Elvis and Colonel Parker make a new partnership agreement, which will split profits 50/50 on live dates

Feb *Movie Stars* publishes an article suggesting Elvis and Linda Thompson will marry, although they are already well on the way to splitting permanently

Apr 20 Elvis invests in Presley Center Courts, Inc., which plans to run racquet-ball clubs, but pulls out when the venture is proved to be losing money

Jul 13 Vernon decides to cut costs and fires Memphis Mafia members Red and Sonny West, and Dave Hebler

Oct 29 Elvis is too ill to work at a recording session at Graceland

Nov 19 Elvis meets another former beauty queen, Ginger Alden, and the following month he gives her a Lincoln Mark V

Dec A 15-concert booking at the Las Vegas Hilton, and Elvis does not miss one. Linda Thompson has left and Ginger Alden is now his official girlfriend

Dec 9 Vernon has a suspected heart attack and is admitted to hospital

1977

Jan *TV Star Parade* publishes an article speculating that Elvis and Priscilla have secretly remarried, but Elvis spends his birthday with Ginger and her sister Rosemary in Palm Springs

Jan 26 Elvis proposes to Ginger, giving her a diamond ring

Feb Elvis takes Ginger to celebrate Lisa Marie's birthday, and the following month he takes Ginger and her family on a 2-week vacation to Hawaii

Apr Elvis collapses during a concert tour and is admitted to the Baptist Memorial Hospital in Memphis

Apr 5 After leaving hospital, Elvis rests at Graceland

May 30 A Boston radio station, WMEX, reports that psychic Gloria James has predicted that Elvis will soon die

Jun 1 Details are announced of a forthcoming CBS concert special, which will be filmed on the next tour

Jul "Way Down"/"Pledging My Love" is released and hits No I in *Billboard*'s Country chart in August. It stays in this chart for 17 weeks, but also spends 21 weeks in the Top 100 chart, reaching No 18, and goes to No 14 on the Easy Listening chart. In the UK it is Elvis's 17th No 1 record

Jul 19 During the *Nine in the Morning Show*, which is broadcast in Los Angeles on KHJ-TV, psychic Jacqueline Eastland predicts that Elvis will soon die

Jul Publication of *Elvis: What Happened?* a book written by Steve Dunleavy, based on material from ex-members of the Memphis Mafia Red West, Sonny West and Dave Hebler

Jul 31 Lisa Marie arrives for a 2-week visit to see her father at Graceland

Aug 1 Philadelphia papers report that psychic Marc Salem also prophesies that Elvis will soon be dead

Aug 16 Elvis is found dead in his bathroom at Graceland. Cause of death is initially given as a heart attack, but the later autopsy cites a drug overdose

Aug 17 Elvis's body lies in state at Graceland, and thousands of fans queue outside to file past the coffin and get one last glimpse of Elvis.

Aug 18 After a funeral held at Graceland, Elvis is laid to rest at Forest Hill Cemetery next to his mother

Aug 23 Vernon signs a contract giving Boxcar Enterprises all rights to the marketing of Elvis-related products.

Aug RCA sell over eight million Elvis records in the six days after his death

Aug 29 Three men try to steal Elvis's body but charges are dropped since they were trying to prove the coffin was empty and that Elvis is still alive

Sep 12 The RIAA certify "Way Down" as Gold

Oct 3 *Elvis in Concert*, a one-hour special that was filmed during the last tour, is shown on CBS-TV

Oct 27 The bodies of both Elvis and his mother are removed from Forest Hill Cemetery. They are reinterred at Graceland, in the Meditation Garden

1978

Jan The entire estate has been left to Lisa Marie, but the trustees soon find that there is no money left

Feb 1 Elvis is posthumously inducted into the *Playboy* Music Hall of Fame

Aug 16–18 Thousands of fans gather outside Graceland on the first anniversary of Elvis's death

1979

Jan Investigations into Elvis's finances reveal that has probably lost millions of dollars in Royalty payments

Feb 11 ABC-TV broadcasts *Elvis*, a biographical movie with Kurt Russell playing Elvis and Shelley Winters as Gladys

Jun 26 Vernon dies of heart failure, and is buried next to Elvis and Gladys

Sep 13 *The Elvis Cover-Up*, which speculates on Elvis's alleged drug addiction and the facts and rumours surrounding his death, is broadcast on ABC-TV

1980

May 8 Elvis's grandmother, Minnie Mae Presley, dies in Memphis

1981

After the IRS claim Elvis's estate owes $14.6 million in inheritance taxes, plus a further $2.3 million in interest. Priscilla plans to open Graceland to the public to raise funds and protect her daughter's inheritance

Jul Courts decide that Boxcar Enterprises has no right to distribute Elvis-related merchandise

1982

Jun 7 The downstairs rooms at Graceland are opened to the public

Oct *The Elvis Medley* is released and goes on to stay in *Billboard*'s Top LPs chart for nine weeks

1984

Elvis is posthumously awarded the first Golden Hat Award from the Academy of Country Music for his influence on country music and the WC Handy Award from the Blues Foundation for "keeping the blues alive"

1986

Feb Elvis is posthumously inducted into the Rock and Roll Hall of Fame in Cleveland, Ohio

1987

BBC TV broadcasts a documentary of Elvis's life, *Elvis, His Life And Times*

At the American Music Awards, Elvis is posthumously awarded an Award of Merit

1988

The 1956 recording of "Hound Dog" is inducted into the NARAS Hall of Fame

Feb 7–8 *Elvis and Me*, a miniseries based on Priscilla's book of her life with Elvis, is broadcast on ABC-TV and becomes the highest-rated TV movie of 1987–88

Oct 4 The *National Enquirer* publishes photographs said to be of Elvis, taken in September 1988

1989

NBC-TV broadcasts *Elvis: Comeback '68* —a repeat of the programme broadcast on Dec 3 1968—which *TV Guide* describes as the best rock performance ever on television

1991

Elvis, The Great Performances (Original Version) is released, a two-volume video collection that features Elvis singing in films, on TV specials and during guest appearances

1992

The two-volume video collection is re-edited and broadcast as *Elvis, The Great Performances (Televised Version)*. Priscilla hosts the broadcast from Graceland. A video, *Elvis, The Lost Performances* is also released, featuring unseen footage from the films of concerts

Jan 22 *The Elvis Conspiracy—The Elvis Files*, is broadcast, a two-hour TV special alleging that Elvis went undercover for the FBI and is actually still alive

Apr 6 The United States postal service decides to issue an Elvis stamp and holds a postcard ballot to chose which image of Elvis is to be used. The image of a young Elvis is the winner.

1993

Feb 1 Since Lisa Marie has turned 25 she is entitled to take charge of her inheritance but instead founds The Elvis Presley Trust to run the estate, with Priscilla and the National Bank of Commerce as co-trustees

1995

The 1956 recording of "Heartbreak Hotel" is inducted into the NARAS Hall of Fame

1997

Aug 16 *Elvis in Concert '97* held at the Mid-South Coliseum in Memphis features Elvis on video accompanied live on stage by over 30 of his former band members and the Memphis Symphony Orchestra. A digitally remastered video is also shown, with Lisa Marie singing "Don't Cry, Daddy" with Elvis

1998

The 1954 recording of "That's All Right, Mama" is inducted into the NARAS Hall of Fame

Elvis is posthumously inducted into the Country Music Hall of Fame

1999

The 1969 recording of "Suspicious Minds" is inducted into the NARAS Hall of Fame

2001

Sep 16 RCA releases a special CD single, "America the Beautiful," which features Elvis singing three songs and has special information that can be accessed when the CD is played on a computer. All proceeds are donated to the American Red Cross Liberty Disaster Relief Fund

Sep 21 "America the Beautiful" enters *Billboard*'s Hot 100 singles Sales Chart at No 8, and peaks at No 6 for two weeks in November

Elvis is posthumously inducted into the Gospel Music Hall of Fame

FILMOGRAPHY

LOVE ME TENDER

Studio: Twentieth Century Fox

Release date: November 15, 1956

Partial cast list: Richard Egan, Debra Paget, Elvis Presley, Robert Middleton, William Campbell, Neville Brand, Mildred Dunnock.

Plot synopsis: *Love Me Tender* is a western drama set immediately after the Civil War. Clint Reno (Elvis) the youngest of the four Reno brothers, has stayed behind to run the family farm during the war, while his older brothers are fighting for the Confederacy. Vance Reno (Richard Egan), the eldest brother whom the family believes to have been killed in battle, returns home to discover that Clint has married Vance's former sweetheart, Cathy (Debra Paget). The plot is further complicated by the Federal Government money that Vance has stolen from a train while in the Confederate Army. Eventually brother is pitted against brother, and Clint dies in Cathy's arms.

LOVING YOU

Studio: Paramount

Release date: July 9, 1957

Partial cast list: Elvis Presley, Lizabeth Scott, Wendell Corey, Dolores Hart, James Gleason, Ralph Dumke, Paul Smith, Ken Becker, Jana Lund

Plot synopsis: Deke (Elvis), a truck driver with a natural talent for singing, teams up with press agent Glenda Markle (Lizabeth Scott), hoping to become the next singing sensation. It soon becomes apparent that the female faction of the audience just can't get enough of Deke either on stage or off. Deke is torn between his attraction to Glenda and his genuine affection for the band's lead singer, Susan (Dolores Hart). When Deke discovers that Glenda has been manipulating him personally and professionally, he is confused and runs away. He returns in time to perform at a major televised concert, which is his introduction to the big time.

JAILHOUSE ROCK

Studio: Metro-Goldwyn-Mayer

Release date: November 8, 1957

Partial cast list: Elvis Presley, Judy Tyler, Mickey Shaughnessy, Vaughn Taylor, Jennifer Holden, Dean Jones, Ann Neyland, Hugh Sanders

Plot synopsis: Vince Everett (Elvis) is sent to prison after being convicted of manslaughter. When his cellmate, country & western singer Hank Houghton (Mickey Shaughnessy), recognizes Vince's singing talent they decide to perform together and share the profit. Once out of jail, Vince tries to get a job as singer, but only achieves success with help from Peggy van Alden (Judy Tyler). They start a record company together, but Vince only seems to be interested in fame and fortune until a confrontation with Hank, who doesn't accept his behavior. During the fight Vince's throat is injured, putting his career in danger. He gets his voice back and realizes the error of his ways.

KING CREOLE

Studio: Paramount

Release date: July 2, 1958

Partial cast list: Elvis Presley, Carolyn Jones, Walther Matthau, Dolores Hart, Dean Jagger, Liliane Montevecchi, Vic Morrow, Paul Stewart, Jan Shepard

Plot synopsis: Danny Fisher (Elvis) sweeps up at a nightclub to earn extra money. One night at the club, Danny runs into gangster's moll Ronnie (Carolyn Jones) and gangster Maxie Fields (Walter Matthau), who insist that he sing. Danny's natural talent attracts the attention of the owner of the King Creole nightspot, who offers him a job. Danny is torn between the love of good girl Nellie (Dolores Hart), and his attraction to the ill-fated Ronnie, and between a singing career and the temptation to join a street gang. A fight with the gang's leader leaves Danny with a serious knife wound and Ronnie nurses him back to health, but jealous Maxie shoots her dead. Maxie in turn is shot by a gang member and Danny returns to singing at the King Creole, reconciled with his family and with Nellie.

G.I. BLUES

Studio: Paramount

Release date: November 23, 1960

Partial cast list: Elvis Presley, Juliet Prowse, Robert Ivers, Leticia Roman, James Douglas, Sigrid Maier, Arch Johnson

Plot synopsis: Tulsa MacLean (Elvis) is an Army sergeant stationed in West Germany, and he and his buddies hope to make enough money to open a small nightclub when they return to civilian life. Tulsa accepts a bet to win the heart of Lili (Juliet Prowse), a beautiful cabaret dancer at the Cafe Europa. Lili has a reputation for resisting soldiers, so Tulsa must break through her cool exterior. He soon realizes that he is in love with Lili, but she finds out that she has been the target of a wager. Later, at a rehearsal for an Armed Forces show, Lili discovers that Tulsa has called off the bet, and realizes he truly loves her.

FLAMING STAR

Studio: Twentieth Century Fox

Release date: December 20, 1960

Partial cast list: Elvis Presley, Steve Forrest, Barbara Eden, Dolores Del Rio, John McIntire, Rudolph Acosta

Plot synopsis: Pacer (Elvis) and Clint (Steve Forrest) Burton arrive at their family ranch for a party held by their parents, Neddy (Dolores Del Rio) and Sam (John McIntire). Their friends the Howards are killed on their return home by a Kiowa war party, led by Buffalo Horn (Rudolpho Acosta). Buffalo Horn arrives at the Burton ranch and asks Pacer to join the Kiowa. He refuses, but he and Neddy go to the Kiowa camp to stop impending disaster. While returning home, Pacer's boyhood friend, Two Moons (Perry Lopez) is killed and Neddy badly injured by Will Howard, who has survived and wants vengeance. Neddy goes to the mountains in search of her "flaming star" of death, and in their grief, Pacer decides to join the Kiowa and Clint to fight the Indians. Clint is badly wounded but Pacer saves him, then rides toward his "flaming star."

WILD IN THE COUNTRY

Studio: Twentieth Century Fox

Release date: June 15, 1961

Partial cast list: Elvis Presley, Hope Lange, Tuesday Weld, Millie Perkins, Rafer Johnson, John Ireland, Gary Lockwood, William Mims, Christina Crawford

Plot synopsis: Glenn Tyler (Elvis) is a young rebel, and after a fight with his drunken brother, who is badly injured, his father rejects him. The court releases Glenn on probation into the care of his uncle in a small town, appointing Irene Sperry (Hope Lange) to give him psychological counseling. Marked out as a troublemaker, Glenn is falsely suspected of various misdemeanors, and also has to choose between his seductive cousin (Tuesday Weld) and his childhood sweetheart (Millie Perkins). The false rumor of an affair between Irene and Glenn causes a scandal, and Irene attempts suicide. Eventually shown to be innocent, Glenn goes off to college to become a writer.

BLUE HAWAII

Studio: Paramount

Release date: November 22, 1961

Partial cast list: Elvis Presley, Joan Blackman, Angela Lansbury, Nancy Walters, Roland Winters, John Archer, Howard McNear, Steve Brodie, Iris Adrian, Hilo Hattie, Jennie Maxwell

Plot synopsis: Chad Gates (Elvis) returns from the army to Hawaii, where his wealthy family owns a successful pineapple plantation. His family wants him to join the family business, but Chad lands a job as a guide in the tourist agency where girlfriend Maile (Joan Blackman) works. This not only allows him to use his knowledge of the Islands' most beautiful sites, but also leaves him plenty of time to mess around on the beach with his native Hawaiian buddies. Chad's blue-blooded mother, (Angela Lansbury), objects to his job, his girlfriend, and his beach-loving friends, and tension begins to mount. However, Chad is a success in the tourist business, and he finally wins the approval of his family by marrying Maile and planning to open his own tourist agency.

FOLLOW THAT DREAM

Studio: United Artists

Release date: April 11, 1962

Partial cast list: Elvis Presley, Arthur O'Connell, Anne Helm, Joanna Moore, Alan Hewitt, Herbert Rudley, Simon Oakland, Howard McNear, Roland Winters

Plot synopsis: The Kwimpers, a family of bumbling rural Southerners—including Toby (Elvis), Pop (Arthur O'Connell), and several adopted orphans—claim squatter's rights on an unopened stretch of highway. They open a small business renting fishing equipment, but gamblers try to take advantage of them. Toby routs the hoods, but beautiful social worker Alicia Claypoole (Joanna Moore), investigates the Kwimpers to determine if the children are receiving proper care. After Toby declines the social worker's amorous advances, Alicia tries to take the children away from Pop Kwimper. Toby and Pop plead their case in a comic courtroom scene, and the judge decides in their favor.

KID GALAHAD

Studio: United Artists

Release date: August 29, 1962

Partial cast list: Elvis Presley, Gig Young, Lola Albright, Joan Blackman, Charles Bronson

Plot synopsis: Boxer Walter Gulick (Elvis) is not a great boxer, but has a powerful right hook and can take a lot of punches. Down-and-out gambler Willy Grogan (Gig Young), who owns the training camp where Walter spars with other boxers, decides to groom Walter to be a professional boxer. He hopes to make enough money to pay off his gambling debts to gangster Otto Danzig (David Lewis). Willy's relationship with Walter changes when Walter fails in love with Willy's sister, Rose (Joan Blackman). Willy does not want Rose to be involved with Walter, so he allows Walter to be overmatched for his next fight by a superior boxer. Just before the big fight, Willy realizes that he has compromised his moral integrity, so he and Walter rid themselves of Danzig and his shady dealings and Walter goes on to win the match.

GIRLS! GIRLS! GIRLS!

Studio: Paramount

Release date: January 16, 1963

Partial cast list: Elvis Presley, Stella Stevens, Jeremy Slate, Laurel Goodwin, Benson Fong, Robert Strauss

Plot synopsis: Ross Carpenter (Elvis) is a charter boat pilot who moonlights as a nightclub singer to buy a sailboat that once belonged to his father. Wealthy Laurel Dodge (Laurel Goodwin), falls hard for Ross and secretly buys the sailboat for him. When Ross discovers that Laurel has purchased the boat, his pride is damaged, and he sails off by himself. Laurel quickly follows in a boat piloted by wealthy Wesley Johnson (Jeremy Slate), who turns out to be a wolf in tailored clothing. Ross rescues Laurel from Wesley's clutches, and realizes that he loves her. He asks Laurel to sell the sailboat, so that he can feel free to marry her and build a new boat.

Elvis on the set of *Love Me Tender*.

IT HAPPENED AT THE WORLD S FAIR

Studio: Metro-Goldwyn-Mayer

Release date: April 3, 1963

Partial cast list: Elvis Presley, Joan O'Brien, Gary Lockwood, Vicky Tiu

Plot synopsis: In this musical comedy filmed against the backdrop of the 1963 Seattle World's Fair, Mike Edwards (Elvis), and partner Danny Burke (Gary Lockwood), hitchhike to Seattle to find work. They desperately need money to reclaim their airplane, which the sheriff is holding against their debts. They hitch a ride with a Chinese farmer and his seven-year-old niece, Sue-Lin (Vicky Tiu). When business unexpectedly occupies the uncle, Mike takes Sue-Lin on a tour of the World's Fair, where he meets and falls for nurse Diane Warren (Joan O'Brien). When Sue-Lin's uncle fails to return Mike takes responsibility for the little girl, but Child Welfare takes Sue-Lin away. Meanwhile, Danny inadvertently becomes involved with a smuggling operation. Mike, Danny, and law officials eventually subdue the smugglers and the movie ends happily when Sue-Lin finds her uncle and Mike and Diane find each other.

FUN IN ACAPULCO

Studio: Paramount

Release date: February 19, 1964

Partial cast list: Elvis Presley, Ursula Andress, Elsa Cardenas, Paul Lukas, Larry Domasin, Alejandro Rey

Plot synopsis: Mike Windgren (Elvis) is a former trapeze artist; his circus career ended when he made a mistake and his partner was seriously injured. Traumatized by the accident, Mike has developed a fear of heights. He finds himself in Acapulco, where he gets a job as a lifeguard at a resort hotel. In the evenings, he entertains the guests by singing. Mike becomes involved with two women—hotel social director Marguerita Dauphin (Ursula Andress), and lady bullfighter Dolores Gomez (Elsa Cardenas). He soon finds himself in competition with another hotel lifeguard, who every night performs a death-defying jump off the ocean cliffs near the hotel. This rival tricks Mike into jumping off the cliffs, but Mike's decision to jump helps him overcome his fears and he decides to spend his life with Marguerita.

Elvis with Joan O'Brien in *It Happened at the World's Fair.*

KISSIN COUSINS

Studio: Metro-Goldwyn-Mayer

Release date: March 6, 1964

Partial cast list: Elvis Presley, Arthur O'Connell, Glenda Farrell, Jack Albertson, Pam Austin, Cynthia Pepper, Yvonne Craig, Maureen Reagan

Plot synopsis: Elvis plays a dual role in Kissin' Cousins. As Air Force officer Josh Morgan, a dark-haired Elvis plays a responsible military man; as blond-haired Jodie Tatum, he appears as a girl-chasin', guntotin' mountain Romeo. Josh has to persuade the Tatums, his distant relatives on his mother's side, to sell their land for a missile site. He runs into his blond-haired double as well as two beautiful country cousins, Azalea (Yvonne Craig) and Selena (Pam Austin). He eventually chooses Azalea—but not before pairing off Selena with his best friend. In the meantime, Jodie takes up with Midge (Cynthia Pepper), a beautiful but fiery WAG. Josh persuades Pappy Tatum to sell one side of his mountain to the government, as long as the military does not interfere with the family's moonshine business on the other side.

VIVA LAS VEGAS

Studio: Metro-Goldwyn-Mayer

Release date: May 20, 1964

Partial cast list: Elvis Presley, Ann-Margret, Cesare Danova, William Demarest, Nicky Blair

Plot synopsis: Lucky Jordan (Elvis) arrives in Las Vegas for the big Grand Prix race, but has engine trouble and needs to find the cash to buy a new engine. He gets a job as a casino waiter and soon earns the money, but falls in love at first sight with Rusty Martin (Ann-Margret). Not knowing her name but assuming she is one of the showgirls, Lucky and his racing rival, Count Elmo Mancini (Cesare Danova), search nightclubs for her. They return to the hotel and spot the girl again—she is the swimming instructor at the hotel pool. Lucky starts singing and romancing her, while also getting his engine put right, in competition with Count Elmo on both accounts. Finally Lucky wins the big race and the girl.

ROUSTABOUT

Studio: Paramount

Release date: November 11, 1964

Partial cast list: Elvis Presley, Barbara Stanwyck, Joan Freeman, Leif Erickson, Sue Ane Langdon, Pat Buttram

Plot synopsis: Charlie Rogers (Elvis), a drifter with a chip on his shoulder, lands a job as a roustabout, or handyman, with a down-and-out carnival operated by strong-willed Maggie Morgan (Barbara Stanwyck). When Charlie breaks into song one day, throngs of young people flock to hear him, and as news of his talent spreads Maggie's carnival begins to turn a profit. Meanwhile a beautiful young carnival worker, Cathy (Joan Freeman), takes a romantic interest in Charlie, but after a misunderstanding involving a customer's missing wallet, Maggie and Cathy both lecture Charlie about his selfish attitudes. Angry and bitter, the young man quits Maggie's outfit to work for a rival. However, when Maggie's carnival starts to go under, Charlie returns with enough money to ward off the creditors, and his unselfish act wins Maggie's respect and Cathy's heart.

GIRL HAPPY

Studio: Metro-Goldwyn-Mayer

Release date: April 14, 1965

Partial cast list: Elvis Presley, Shelley Fabares, Harold J. Stone, Gary Crosby, Joby Baker, Nita Talbot, Mary Ann Mobley, Fabrizio Mioni, Jackie Coogan, Jimmy Hawkins

Plot synopsis: Rusty Wells (Elvis) is a struggling pop singer, whose musical combo works for a tough Chicago nightclub owner known as Big Frank (Harold J. Stone).

Big Frank's big weakness is his only daughter Valerie (Shelley Fabares), who insists on spending her Easter vacation on the beaches of sunny, sinful Fort Lauderdale. Frank sends Rusty and his friends to Florida to keep an eye on Valerie without her knowing about it. Once there, Rusty attempts to pursue a few girls of his own, but is constantly interrupted by the need to rescue Valerie from various local lover boys. Inevitably, Valerie falls in love with the smooth-talking Rusty.

TICKLE ME

Studio: Allied Artists

Release date: June 30, 1965

Partial cast list: Elvis Presley, Julie Adams, Jocelyn Lane, Jack Mullaney, Merry Anders, Bill Williams, Edward Faulkner

Plot synopsis: Lonnie Beale (Elvis) is a singing rodeo cowboy, who moonlights as a handyman at a beauty spa. Although several women try to catch his attention—including spa owner Vera Radford (Julie Adams), the rodeo rider falls for Pam Merritt (Jocelyn Lane). Pam is visiting the spa to investigate a nearby ghost town where her grandfather has supposedly hidden a cache of gold. She enlists the help of Lonnie and his sidekick Stanley (Jack Mullaney) to recover the treasure. Unscrupulous locals, also looking for the gold, try to frighten the three of them into leaving the territory but finally they discover the cache. Lonnie and Pam marry at the end—one of the few times that Elvis's character actually weds on-screen.

HARUM SCARUM

Studio: Metro-Goldwyn-Mayer

Release date: November 24, 1965

Partial cast list: Elvis Presley, Mary Ann Mobley, Fran Jeffries, Michael Ansara, Jay Novello, Philip Reed, Theo Marcuse, Billy Barty

Plot synopsis: Matinee idol Johnny Tyronne (Elvis) is a famous movie and recording star who makes the women swoon and the men jealous. On tour in Lunarkand—a fictional country in the Middle East—Johnny is kidnapped by a gang of assassins and thrust into a plot to kill King Toranshah (Philip Reed). Johnny escapes and falls in with a band of pickpockets and rogues, while rescuing damsels in distress and singing songs. Johnny falls in love with a beautiful handmaiden (Mary Ann Mobley); although he doesn't know it, she is really Princess Shalimar, daughter of King Toranshah. Johnny thwarts the assassination attempt on the king, wins the heart of Princess Shalimar, and returns to America with a new act; he opens in Las Vegas with a Middle Eastern dancing troupe, complete with exotic harem girls.

FRANKIE AND JOHNNY

Studio: United Artists

Release date: March 31, 1966

Partial cast list: Elvis Presley, Donna Douglas, Harry Morgan, Sue Ane Langdon, Nancy Kovack, Audrey Christie, Robert Strauss

Plot synopsis: In the original the folk song "Frankie and Johnny" the title characters are lovers whose romance goes wrong when Nellie Bly steals Johnny and Frankie shoots him dead. In this lighthearted version, the song has been specially written for riverboat performers Frankie (Donna Douglas) and Johnny (Elvis). Johnny is a gambler whose bad luck changes when dancer Nellie Bly (Nancy Kovack) joins the riverboat. Each night, the three perform the number "Frankie and Johnny" onstage, but as Johnny's interest in Nellie increases Frankie becomes jealous. Someone loads real bullets into Frankie's prop gun, and Johnny is shot during the performance, but is saved by a charm that he wears around his neck.

PARADISE HAWAIIAN STYLE

Studio: Paramount

Release date: June 15, 1966

Partial cast list: Elvis Presley, Suzanna Leigh, James Shigeta, Donna Butterworth, Marianna Hill, Irene, TSU, Linda Wong, Julie Parrish, Jan Shepard

Plot synopsis: Greg "Rick" Richards (Elvis) is a helicopter pilot running a charter service in Hawaii with his friend Danny (James Shigeta). Beautiful Judy Hudson (Suzanna Leigh) runs their office, and Danny fears that Rick will not be able to resist her so he tells him that their "Girl Friday" is married. A misunderstanding involving a forced helicopter landing leads to Rick having his license temporarily suspended by the Federal Aviation Agency (FAA). Rick risks his license to rescue Danny and his daughter from a deserted island, but the FAA understands the mitigating circumstances surrounding Rick's decision and rules that he will be able to fly again. In the meantime, Rick discovers that Judy is not married, and the two begin a romance.

Elvis in *Frankie and Johnny*.

SPINOUT

Studio: Metro-Goldwyn-Mayer

Release date: November 23, 1966

Partial cast list: Elvis Presley, Shelley Fabares, Diane McBain, Deborah Walley, Dodie Marshall, Jack Mullaney, Will Hutchins, Warren Berlinger, Jimmy Hawkins, Carl Betz

Plot synopsis: Dashing Mike McCoy (Elvis) fronts a popular singing group and is also defending champion on the racing circuit. Fast cars are less dangerous for Mike than beautiful women, all of whom want to race him down the aisle to marriage. Les (Deborah Walley) is the drummer in Mike's band and is jealous of his attention toward other women. Also vying for Mike's affection is sophisticated Cynthia Foxhugh (Shelley Fabares), the daughter of a wealthy auto magnate and writer Diana St. Clair (Diane McBain). Mike does not end up marrying any of these women; instead, he succeeds in wedding them off to friends and associates, while he remains free to begin a new romance.

EASY COME, EASY GO

Studio: Paramount

Release date: March 22, 1967

Partial cast list: Elvis Presley, Dodie Marshall, Pat Priest, Pat Harrington, Jr., Skip Ward, Elsa Lanchester, Frank McHugh

Plot synopsis: Navy frogman Ted Jackson (Elvis) is about to be discharged from the service, but finds a treasure chest on a sunken ship. Captain Jack (Frank McHugh), a local expert on nautical lore, is unable to tell Ted about the ship's cargo, but knows the name of the captain's only descendant, Jo Symington (Dodie Marshall). Jo believes the chest contains pieces-of-eight and agrees to help Ted if the money is given to the community arts center. Their attempts to retrieve the treasure are impeded by scoundrels Gil Carey (Skip Ward) and Dina Bishop (Pat Priest), who steal Ted's equipment and kidnap Captain Jack. Ted tracks them down and rescues Jack, but when the chest is opened the coins are found to be copper, not gold. Ted donates the money for a down payment on a new arts center, and wins Jo's heart.

DOUBLE TROUBLE

Studio: Metro-Goldwyn-Mayer

Release date: April 5, 1967

Partial cast list: Elvis Presley, Annette Day, John Williams, Yvonne Romain, Harry Wiere, Herbert Wiere, Sylvester Wiere

Plot synopsis: Guy Lambert (Elvis) is a pop singer who goes on tour to Antwerp and is followed by beautiful heiress Jill Conway (Annette Day), who has a crush on him—much to the annoyance of her guardian. Jewel thieves hide smuggled diamonds in Jill's luggage and she leads Guy through numerous adventures involving the jewel thieves, spies, counterspies, and a pair of harebrained detectives (Harry and Herbert Wiere). A sexy society sophisticate, Claire Dunham (Yvonne Romain) is also interested in Guy, but eventually Jill succeeds in catching his attention, and the two marry.

CLAMBAKE

Studio: United Artists

Release date: November 22, 1967

Partial cast list: Elvis Presley, Shelley Fabares, Will Hutchins, Bill Bixby, James Gregory, Gary Merrill

Plot synopsis: Scott Heyward (Elvis), the son of a multi-millionaire, meets poor but happy Tom Wilson (Will Hutchins), who is on his way to begin a new job as a water skiing instructor. The two agree to trades places—Scott is eager to be accepted for himself and not his money, while Tom wants to try out the lifestyle that money can bring. Scott meets Dianne (Shelley Fabares) who is trying to land a rich husband. When playboy James Jamison (Bill Bixby) catches Dianne's eye, she asks Scott to help her catch him. Scott agrees, but finds himself attracted to her. Meanwhile, Scott repairs a radically-designed speedboat for a race that's going to take place at the hotel, and ends up winning the race and getting the girl.

STAY AWAY, JOE

Studio: Metro-Goldwyn-Mayer

Release date: March 8, 1968

Partial cast list: Elvis Presley, Burgess Meredith, Joan Blondell, Katy Jurado, Thomas Gomez, Henry Jones, L.Q. Jones, Quentin Dean

Plot synopsis: Rodeo rider Joe Lightcloud (Elvis), is a Navajo whose family still lives on the reservation. Joe persuades his congressman to give him 20 heifers and a prize bull so he and his father (Burgess Meredith) can prove that the Navajos can successfully raise cattle on the reservation. If their experiment is successful, the government will help all the Navajo people. However, Joe's buddy accidentally barbecues the prize bull, while Joe sells the heifers to buy plumbing and other home improvements for his stepmother (Katy Jurado). Meanwhile Marnie Callahan (Quentin Dean), daughter of a local tavern owner (Joan Blondell) can't seem to stay away from the girl-chasing Joe.

Elvis with Nancy Sinatra in *Speedway*.

SPEEDWAY

Studio: Metro-Goldwyn-Mayer

Release date: June 12, 1968

Partial cast list: Elvis Presley, Nancy Sinatra, Bill Bixby, Gale Gordon, William Schallert, Victoria Meyerink

Plot synopsis: Stockcar champion Steve Grayson (Elvis), is a generous soul who is always sharing his winnings with people in need. Partly due to his generosity and partly because his manager Kenny Donford (Bill Bixby) loves gambling, Steve finds himself owing the government back taxes. IRS agent Susan Jacks (Nancy Sinatra) attempts to put Steve on a budget that will allow him to pay off the government in installments. Steve tries to soften the all-business agent with romance and music, but she thinks him frivolous and irresponsible. However, her tune changes when she realizes that Steve's latest charity case is a former stock-car driver with five daughters who has fallen on hard times. Eventually Susan is able to keep Steve on a budget, and Steve is able to win Susan's heart.

LIVE A LITTLE, LOVE A LITTLE

Studio: Metro-Goldwyn-Mayer

Release date: October 23, 1968

Partial cast list: Elvis Presley, Michele Carey, Don Porter, Rudy Vallee, Dick Sargent, Sterling Holloway, Celeste Yarnall

Plot synopsis: Greg Nolan (Elvis) is a newspaper photographer who has a fun-filled and carefree life until he meets oddball Bernice (Michele Carey). Bernice switches names and personalities whenever the mood takes her, and she loses Greg both his job and his apartment. She manages to get him a new apartment, but it is so expensive that Greg has to take on two full-time jobs to make the payments. As Greg hustles back and forth between the two photography jobs—one for a stuffy conservative publisher, and the other for a "girlie" magazine—he still finds time to romance beautiful model Ellen (Celeste Yarnall).

CHARRO!

Studio: National General

Release date: March 13, 1969

Partial cast list: Elvis Presley, Ina Balin, Victor French, Lynn Kellogg, Barbara Werle, Soloman Sturges, Paul Brinegar, James Sikking

Plot synopsis: In this offbeat western with no musical numbers Jess Wade (Elvis), a reformed badman, is pitted against the members of his old gang. The gang is now led by Vince Hackett (Victor French), and they have stolen a small Mexican town's prized gold-plated cannon, which was used by Emperor Maximilian in his ill-fated fight against popular Mexican leader Benito Juarez. The gang plan to extort a ransom from the town for the cannon, but they also use it to hold the townspeople at bay. Wade is accused of stealing the cannon himself, and has to tackle his former gang to take it back and prove his innocence. Tracy Winters (Ina Balin) is a dance hall hostess in love with Wade.

THE TROUBLE WITH GIRLS

Studio: Metro-Goldwyn-Mayer

Release date: September 3, 1969

Partial cast list: Elvis Presley, Marlyn Mason, Nicole Jaffe, Sheree North, Edward Andrews, John Carradine, Vincent Price, Anissa Jones, Joyce Van Patten, Pepe Brown, Dabney Coleman

Plot synopsis: Walter Hale (Elvis) is the manager of a traveling Chautauqua—a school that provides education combined with entertainment. Walter is worrying about several problems as his show arrives in town for one week; he might have to give the mayor's untalented daughter the lead in the children's pageant to stay in the mayor's good graces, and he has to deal with his assistant, Charlene (Marlyn Mason), who is constantly nagging him about the union rights of his employees. However, these problems fade into insignificance when someone murders the local druggist, and a member of the Chautauqua is accused. All is resolved during the final show, when Walter reveals the killer's identity and wins the heart of his pretty assistant.

CHANGE OF HABIT

Studio: Universal

Release date: November 10, 1969

Partial cast list: Elvis Presley, Mary Tyler Moore, Barbara McNair, Jane Elliot, Leora Dana, Edward Asner, Robert Emhardt, Regis Toomey, Doro Merande, Ruth McDevitt, Richard Carlson, Nefti Millet, Laura Figueroa, Lorena Kirk, Virgina Vincent, The Blossoms

Plot synopsis: Dr. John Carpenter (Elvis) heads a clinic in a ghetto area of a major city and is surprised to be offered assistance by three women. Although he does not know it, the y are nuns in street clothing who want to help the community, but are afraid local residents might be reluctant to seek help from a nun. Carpenter falls in love with Sister Michelle Gallagher (Mary Tyler Moore), still not knowing that she is a nun. Sister Michelle also has feelings for the doctor, but she is reluctant to leave the order. The movie concludes with Sister Michelle entering a church to pray for guidance to make her choice—the church or Dr. Carpenter.

CONCERT MOVIES

ELVIS, THAT S THE WAY IT IS

Studio: Metro-Goldwyn-Mayer

Release date: November 11, 1970

ELVIS ON TOUR

Studio: Metro-Goldwyn-Mayer

Release date: November 1, 1972

TELEVISION SPECIALS

ELVIS (also known as the Comeback Special)

NBC-TV

First transmission date: December 3, 1968

ELVIS: ALOHA FROM HAWAII

Live via satellite

First transmission date: January 14, 1973

ELVIS IN CONCERT

CBS

First transmission date: October 3, 1977

Acknowledgments

The photographs in this book are courtesy of Getty Images.

Thanks to Hayley Newman, Rick Mayston, Patricia Froux-Leaker, Stacey Smithson, Martina Oliver, Hilary Marsden, Cliff Salter and John Dunne.